ADVANCE PRAISE FOR *LONG-TERM THINKING FOR A SHORT-SIGHTED WORLD*

"THIS BOOK IS LONG OVERDUE. THIS MAY HELP BRING together those who are really interested in finding long-term solutions for sustainability for all the world's people."

Jacque Fresco
The Venus Project

"We have read a lot of books, watched numerous documentaries and sat through countless talks on sustainability. Jim Brumm's book, *Long-Term Thinking for a Short-Sighted World*, represents the best presentation of this type of information we have ever come across in any kind of media. Brumm helps us to understand that the need for 'sacrificing' short-term desire for long-term needs is not a sacrifice at all; it brings a sense of relief and peace while providing opportunities for generations to come. Using simple-to-understand, straightforward language, Brumm has taken the many challenges we face today and shown us that they share a common thread: a lack of long-term thinking."

Tara Smith
Tara Firma Farms

"If you read only one book this year let it be Jim Brumm's *Long Term Thinking For a Short-Sighted World.*" Brumm speaks with a gentle voice but his words will cut you to the quick because, step by step, rationally, and with great care, they expose the folly of modern living and the disaster toward which we're heading unless, as a species, we choose to change. Brumm shows how everything we do is aimed at quick gratification, short-term reward—an endless, blind grasping for more and more. How to overcome this mindless addiction for growth and gain? By looking at the grand scheme of things, at the long, slow, deep, self-sustaining cycles of nature of which, ultimately, and inextricably, we are a part. Somehow—and quickly—we must reach bedrock, get back in touch with the planet and with our communal consciousness. Brumm offers a plan, not difficult in principle, for us to save the Earth's ecosystem, in all its wonderful diversity, by taking the long view and moving back into harmony with the world around us."

David Darling
Astronomer and author of *Equations on Eternity*

"Jim Brumm's new book, *Long-Term Thinking for a Short-Sighted World*, is a happy signpost on the way to restoring much-needed balance and sanity to our lives and our planet. This book offers a chance to slow down, reflect and regroup as we plan for a future rooted in sustainable, long-term visioning and action. As Brumm says in his book, 'We can start, when faced with a problem, whether a petty argument at work or a global crisis, by asking this simple question: How can I make this better?' Brumm's book offers profound inspiration and perspective on how we each can make things better."

Deborah McNamara
Director of Organizational Partnerships,
Northwest Earth Institute
ww.nwei.org

"IN LONG-TERM THINKING FOR A SHORT-SIGHTED WORLD, Jim Brumm takes us on a poignant journey starting from a time when we lived in balance with nature to where we are today. Throughout his writing, Jim brings to light facts that we are all aware of on one level or another but choose to ignore. Brumm points out that we cannot look to the government or big business to fix the mess that we are in—we need to wake up, take an honest look at the bigger picture and change the way we think and live. A must read to help us all return to a sane world."

Grace Aroha
www.GracefulExchange.org

Long-Term Thinking for a Short-Sighted World

JIM BRUMM

Muse Harbor Publishing
Los Angeles • Santa Barbara

Long-Term Thinking For A Short-Sighted World

A Muse Harbor Publishing Book

PUBLISHING HISTORY

Muse Harbor Publishing paperback edition published July 2012

Published by Muse Harbor Publishing, Inc

Los Angeles, California

Santa Barbara, California

Cover design by Dave Workman

ISBN 978-1-61264-124-9

Visit our website at

http://www.museharbor.com

v1.0

To my mother, Patricia Brumm,

who showed me the way.

ACKNOWLEDGEMENTS

IT ALL STARTED WITH LUNCH AT A CHINESE RESTAU-rant in Santa Rosa, California. I was meeting my long-time friend, Elizabeth Slater—E, as she's known to her friends—to visit and catch up. Before I arrived I had heard a newscast about what I considered a bad decision made by our congress, a decision that would harm the planet, but save jobs. When I arrived at the restaurant I barely sat down before I started ranting about our political process. "I can't believe how short-sighted people can be!" I went on in this way for some time. E listened patiently and worked on her meal. When I finally stopped to draw breath, she looked at me and calmly said, "You have a book in this, you know."

I didn't take her comment seriously at the time, but it stuck in my head and I began thinking about the subject of long-term thinking all the time. Finally, I bought a notebook and began jotting down every thought I had, no matter how obscure, that might relate to the subject. I researched and discovered how few books there were that spoke directly to long-term thinking. Two-and-a-half years later, here it is. Thank you E, for listening to my rant, and opening my eyes—for seeing what I couldn't. I will be forever grateful.

LET'S HAVE LUNCH.

When you embark on a book-writing project, you invariably draw those close to you into the vortex of your obsession. I did not write this book alone. I could not have done it without others who helped me through the hard times every writer faces, those times when we look up from the keyboard and ask: What have I gotten myself into? Who do I think I am? Who would ever want to read this? To write a book is to live in your head for a long time, mulling over what you said, trying to find a way to say it better.

For a couple of years now I have been asked by everyone I know, everywhere I go, "How's the book coming?" Many people lent me their support with their interest and excitement for the idea, and I am grateful to them all for keeping me motivated and convinced that there was great interest in the subject. I hope my efforts rise to their expectations.

I would like to thank my mother, Patricia Brumm, a long-time editor, who gave me my love of reading and passion for the written word. She helped me clarify my thinking, talked me through difficult concepts on frequent phone calls, and let me know when my smartass personality went too far in my writing. She walked with me through every word of every line of every chapter, with love, infinite patience and boundless enthusiasm. My entire life she has given me the gift of believing that it is possible. My gift in return is to show her that she was right.

Thanks to my wonderful wife, Theresa Stoops, whose unwavering support and belief in me, even when I wasn't sure I deserved it, carried me through to the end. On long walks along the creek, on weekend mornings over coffee, on drives to the coast with the top down, and pretty much any time I could get her to listen to me, she made this journey with me through my struggles and successes. Together we dreamed, laughed, and pondered. She pointed out flaws in my thinking, and offered suggestions and insights I hadn't thought of, rooting me on patiently, and listening to each chapter as I read them aloud to her. I would not have succeeded in finishing this without her. Her love and presence in my life is my rock.

Thank you to Vivien Straus, Bob Canning, Lisa Consani, and Lorie DeLap—my fellow members of *The Scribs*, by far the greatest writing group in the world. For a writer, finding a good writer's group can make all the difference, and ours is surely the best anywhere. Our weekly meetings in Petaluma have become a part of my life, and all of you have become extended family to me. I don't know what I would have done without your support, criticism, laughter and enthusiasm, all delivered while eating french fries off each other's plates. Here's to vanquishing the blank page together.

Thank you to my friend, Tim Laughlin, who spent countless hours talking about this book idea and the concept of long-term thinking with me, and who brilliantly conceived and laid out the road trip through time in chapter two.

Thank you to my sons, Paul and Andrew, for your love, support, ideas, great conversations and inspiration over the years.

Thanks to my sister Susan, and brother John, who both took the time to read chapters and offer suggestions as I went along. Our discussions helped me stay enthusiastic and focused.

Thank you to my publishers, Ian Wood, Eileen and Dave Workman, and the crew at Muse Harbor Publishing, who believed in my work and gave me the opportunity to share it with the world.

And finally, thanks to my editor, Matt Pallamary, who took my work and transformed it into something clearer, tighter and much better. His skill and guidance taught me more about writing than I had learned in a lifetime.

Contents

INTRODUCTION

In today's world we are grappling at every turn with increasing energy shortages, food production systems that struggle to feed increasing millions, environmental problems that threaten our survival, a debt crisis that is crippling individuals and governments, and so much more. All of these problems come with their own unique challenges and examined on their own they may seem completely different from each other, but they share one common, rarely discussed hidden thread that runs through the center of each and binds them together: *a lack of long-term thinking.*

We're very bad long-term thinkers.

The human race lives in fear of death and scarcity and will almost always take the shortest, easiest route to gratify short-term needs without considering the possible long term results, inevitably leading to long-term consequences that we might have avoided if we had given the original decision more thought.

Though today's problems seem endemic to our modern era, most are not new at all. A cursory look at recorded history reveals a plethora of examples of civilizations—including ours—that created huge problems due to short-term thinking. It seems there is a basic quirk in the way our minds are wired; a quirk that worked in the distant past but doesn't serve us well in modern times.

Our short-term thinking not only adversely affects big things like our environment; it also affects how we live out each day, how we treat others, our buying decisions, and the story we tell ourselves about who we are. Additionally it affects how we see the world, our place in it, and how susceptible we are to the manipulation and fear mongering of leaders and corporations.

As a result of our shortsightedness we are overfeeding the present by stealing from the future. If we're going to survive we need to make a drastic change in the way we perceive our lives and our place in the stream of time, how we relate to each other, what we prioritize, and how we go about meeting our basic needs. We need to enlarge our image of who we are to embrace all of humanity, not just our tribe, our race or our country. We need to expand our consciousness enough to intelligently and thoughtfully project the consequences of our actions far into the future, using our collective and individual wisdom and experience to anticipate problems and take measures to head them off. We need to plan our actions, large and small, with built-in safety margins, giving ourselves time and room to make corrections when unforeseen problems arise.

We need to think long term. Not just for the next five years, or 20, but for the next 100 years, 500 years, 1000 years and beyond.

It's time to reevaluate our priorities, what happiness means, and which things in life actually matter and serve us in the long run. It's a matter of acknowledging that the way we currently do things cannot be kept up indefinitely. As our knowledge and technology advance beyond our ability to control the situations and things we create, we must do the work required to think in the long term or we will find our future as a species to be very short term.

There is a growing awareness that greed and profit causes great harm to the global economy. Our endless pursuit of wealth and growth has created more hardship and heartache than happiness and satisfaction. *We have reached a point of diminishing returns*, yet we continue to put huge amounts of energy into trying to "fix" our systems using the old way of thinking, hoping for different results. This doesn't work, and on some level we all know that. It's time to re-envision our future and our present using a different model, one that not only satisfies the needs of the present but also anticipates and nurtures our future and that of our descendants.

In this book we will look at the problems we've caused through our short-term thinking and investigate the choices that brought us to where we are today. We'll examine our faulty long-term thinking and see how it is partly inherent and partly foisted on us; we'll explore what really matters and what brings us happiness, security and satisfaction in the long run. It's obvious that what we've been doing doesn't work anymore, but if we think long term and work together we can find a better way. It's a matter of shifting our consciousness, embracing the big picture, and getting out of our own way.

1

THE BORNEO CAT DROP AND THE RISE OF SHORT-TERM THINKING

Unlike many other laws, the laws of nature are all strictly enforced.

Ashleigh Brilliant

Whenever science makes a discovery, the devil grabs it while the angels are debating the best way to use it.

Alan Valentine

IN THE EARLY 1950S, MALARIA HAD BROKEN OUT in parts of Borneo. The World Health Organization went in and carpeted the problem areas with the new miracle state-of-the-art pesticide, DDT, to kill the mosquitoes that carried that disease. The DDT killed the mosquitoes and reduced cases of malaria, but it also killed the population of a local wasp that fed on a caterpillar that fed on the thatch that the locals used to build the roofs on their homes. Without wasps to keep them in check, the caterpillar population exploded. Suddenly, inexplicably, peoples' roofs began collapsing.

The local population of geckoes ate the insects poisoned with DDT, absorbing the chemical into their own bodies. The geckoes were caught and eaten by the local cat population, which absorbed the DDT from the geckoes and began dying in droves. Once the cats were gone, the rat population, carrying disease-laden fleas, boomed, bringing an outbreak of typhus and plague, far more dangerous and deadly than the malaria the people were originally dealing with. Finally, desperate to bring the whole circular fiasco to a close, the Royal Air Force airdropped cats into the villages of Borneo to stave off the rats. Eventually things stabilized and returned to a modicum of normalcy. If it weren't so tragic, this Keystone-Cop–like episode would be funny.

The Borneo Cat Drop is a classic example of what happens when humans approach a problem using short-term thinking. Unfortunately, short-term thinking is how we approach nearly everything. We see a symptom and we react to the symptom only, ignoring the system as a whole when whole system thinking is what's needed. This leads to unforeseen consequences such as those the people of Borneo experienced. History, and our world today, is rife with stories like the Borneo Cat Drop.

In Indonesia, efforts to save wild, ground-nesting birds in the area included a campaign to eradicate the large feral cat population that had been killing the birds. The cats were killed, leading to an explosion in the local rabbit population. The rabbits, with no predators to keep them in check, proceeded to eat all of the vegetation—vegetation that the ground-nesting birds needed for their nests.

In the 1980s, volunteer scuba divers in Southern California converged on the rich kelp beds growing offshore. Spiny sea urchins that fed on the holdfasts—the part of the kelp plants that keep them fixed to the rocks—had grown in population until the kelp forests themselves were threatened. The sea urchin population had exploded because we'd killed all the predators that kept them in check. These altruistic divers took little hammers down with them, and spent the morning smashing thousands and thousands of sea urchins in an unprecedented echinoderm slaughter. What these kelp-loving divers failed to take into consideration is that sea urchins reproduce by releasing sperm and eggs directly into the sea, counting on currents and destiny to match the two up. As the divers smashed their urchin victims to save their beloved kelp, the sea around them became thick with the perfect recipe to create millions of new urchins, all eager to grow up and eat lots of kelp.

In 1890, Eugene Schieffelin, a member of the New York Genealogical and Biographical Society, and apparently a big fan of William Shakespeare, decided it would be a good idea to release into the skies of New York all the birds mentioned in the Bard's plays, including the European Starling. He set 60 starlings imported from England free in Central Park, along with 40 other bird species, many of which didn't thrive in the New World. The starlings, however, did just fine. Today, it is estimated that from those original 60 birds, the starling population throughout the United States surpasses 200 million and has pushed other native species out, causing billions of dollars in lost crops from one end of the country to the other.

Schieffelin was also a member of the Acclimation Society of North America, formed with the misguided goal of promoting the exchange of animals and plants from one part of the world to another. The group meant well; at that time little was known of the problems that would be created by what have come to be known as invasive species.

Today the world faces many environmental problems, some of them bordering on catastrophes, because of our collective inability or unwillingness to think things through. When we are faced with a problem or want to change something in our lives or environment for any reason, we tend to focus on what is in front of us, losing sight of the big picture. This tendency seems to be ubiquitous to humanity, cutting across borders, cultures and time. Our lives are short. It's difficult to project the consequences of our actions into the future. What we think of as a long time turns out to be a very short time indeed. Nature works on a slow, lumbering scale.

Ten thousand years, about how long it's been since the last ice age, about the time people first began experimenting with planting crops, is a proverbial blink of an eye in deep time. To us, in our personal experience and short life spans, 10,000 years seems a very long time. Not only is it difficult to visualize time on nature's scale, we aren't motivated to do so in the first place. We evolved in a world that rewarded right-now thinking, or at least didn't punish it. Early humans, living in small, hunter-gatherer bands for hundreds of thousands of years had scarce reasons to think much further than the next meal. When an organism, whether it's a dodo bird, a ferret, a mushroom, or a human, evolves in one set of circumstances, it develops survival skills and adaptations that favor those original circumstances. When circumstances change, that organism needs to evolve to meet the new challenges or face extinction.

Watch a squirrel cross the road. Run, run, run, freeze. Run, run, freeze, turn around and run back a little, freeze. Turn around again and run, run, run, freeze. Smack. A car hits him and a hundred million years of finely honed evolution goes out the window. This behavior worked in an environment where the only things that were trying to kill squirrels relied on motion to spot their prey. That's why they do it. All the successful squirrels through history did the run-and-stop thing when they moved across open space, but this factory-installed evolutionary trait is a disadvantage to squirrels trying to deal with something like crossing a road, something evolution did not prepare them for. Likewise, our short-term outlook worked great for thousands of years, but is a liability in today's modern world where things move fast and decisions have far-reaching ramifications around the globe and over time.

Humans have come a long way since the first hunter-gatherers converged on the edge of the African savannah and began puzzling things out. Our large, inquisitive minds enabled us to create, invent and modify our environment to meet our needs, but the lesson that has been slow in coming is that every time we change something we change something else, because everything is connected. *Everything.* It's often difficult to see these connections, but everything we do affects everything else. Spray for malaria and the roof falls in. Who knew?

We didn't always mess up everything we touched. For hundreds of thousands of years humans lived like all the other animals on Earth. We hunted for food, got hunted for food, gathered plants, had a few laughs and died. Like good campers we left things the way we found them. If we all gathered our stuff at any particular moment and walked away from a particular area—which we did all the time—you couldn't tell we had been there at all. The next generation did the same followed by the next, and on and on. This continued unaltered for time spans we have difficulty conceptualizing, for millions of years.

Over time humans traveled out of our birthplace in Africa to wander into the Middle East, then on to Asia and Europe. Living in small bands, we adapted to a wide range of climate conditions, food sources, and terrains. Our early ancestors did not live in a state of food insecurity, scratching out a meager subsistence-level diet. Starvation did not nip at their heels. On the contrary, having evolved and learned the ways of the land over millennia, they knew what was good to eat, where to find it and when it was available. The passed this knowledge down through countless generations.

Humans have always possessed the one trait necessary for long-term survival: adaptability. For millennia we have lived through many climate changes, from ice ages to droughts. We saw the landscape change, herds come and go, shorelines recede and advance; and we survived it all. We have co-existed with wooly mammoths, saber-toothed tigers, giant sloths and the rest of the ice-age animals we see in museums and movies. We were (and are) clever and tough.

Unlike today's remaining hunter-gatherer societies, who by modern standards are poor and desperate and generally unwelcome when they come too close to our towns, our early hunter-gatherer ancestors were not marginalized and forced to live off the most unyielding and unproductive land. They could nestle deeply into the most rich and bountiful areas they could find. By many accounts, food gathering took a small about of their available time, leaving lots of time for play or ceremony. Hunter-gatherer groups then and today are largely egalitarian, sharing resources and food equally among their members. Ownership was not a priority. We didn't gather possessions that had to be lugged around on our travels. Anything we needed could be created and disposed of wherever we were, and created anew at our next stop.

This way of life also limited our population. Only so many could be supported and sustained this way. Babies had to be carried and there were natural limits to how much food a particular environment could provide. This balance of population and food availability lasted for most of the two million or so years of early human and modern human existence. We lived this way for over 99 percent of the time we've been around as a species. Just as successive bands of gorillas, prides of lions or pods of whales today can exist for thousands of generations without altering their environment, humans too lived lightly on the planet, taking only what was needed while leaving an occasionally fossilized bone or stone tool for some inquisitive person to ponder thousands of years in the future. Things were working out just fine until about 12,000 or so years ago when a few clever souls living at the tail end of the last ice age thought they'd try out some revolutionary ideas, and things began to change rapidly.

A caveman and a cavewoman are sitting around the fire playing truth or dare.

"Truth or dare?" the caveman asks the cavewoman.

She thinks for a moment and answers, "Truth."

The caveman smiles and moves closer to her. "What's your biggest fantasy?" he whispers.

The cavewoman lowers her eyes, licks her lips suggestively and answers, "Agriculture."

Often referred to as the first great transition in human history, the discovery of agriculture changed everything not only for humans but for other species as well, along with entire ecosystems. This was a seriously huge leap that changed how we lived, how we related to our environment, each other, and how we saw ourselves in relation to the rest of nature. Ultimately it will force us to make some hard choices about our future and the future of those who succeed us. After two million years—bang—everything changed.

Agriculture developed from a series of experiments and attempts over time that rapidly shifted the way we do things. It took many generations, and each of those didn't see anything too radical happen at once, but it added up. Around the same time, from 12,000 to 10,000 years ago, people all over the world had inklings of the same idea and began experimenting with different forms of agriculture, tending those plants they preferred and excluding those they didn't.

Humans settled down, adopting what evolutionary anthropologists and archeologists call sedentism, and from there things progressed quickly. We learned to domesticate animals, which increased our food security even more. Over the next several thousand years the paradigm of how humans lived was transformed so dramatically that the customs of the previous two million years faded into the past in favor of the new ways.

As a dependable food-producing system, agriculture provided a steady food source close by and, for the first time in history, made it possible for a society to support large numbers of people not directly involved in food procurement, such as artisans, religious leaders, craftsmen, soldiers, and (God help us!) bureaucrats and government officials.

In an article in *Discover* magazine, writer Jared Diamond called the discovery of agriculture "the worst mistake in the history of the human race," pointing out that agriculture limited our diets, created malnutrition, created more work for everyone and encouraged the spread of infectious diseases and parasites. After agriculture came along, life for most got harder, not easier.

Once we got the agriculture ball rolling it couldn't be stopped, as Clive Ponting pointed out in his book, *A New Green History of the World*. Every advance in agriculture acted like a ratchet, clicking to the next level, precluding ever going back to the old ways. Once the population grew past a certain point it prevented a return to the hunter-gatherer lifestyle. The extra people could not be fed, individuals had acquired too many possessions and our basic leadership and social hierarchy changed, and those age-old hunter-gatherer skills began to wane over time.

The human population grew, and grew quickly. Now that they didn't have to carry them around and there was a steady food supply, women bore more children. Human population, which had remained steady for hundreds of thousands of years, could now expand as large as the available food would allow. It is estimated that 12,000 years ago the population of the entire world was between three and a half and four million. It took two million years to reach that level. From that point forward it grew exponentially, reaching around 50 million by 1000 BCE, just 11 thousand years later. With a few ups and downs over the years, it's been growing ever since. We never looked back. Today, farmers worldwide struggle to sustain a still-growing population of seven billion people.

Of course if you're growing your food, you have to tend it. For agriculture to succeed people had to invest extensive time and energy into their crops. By necessity the first villages formed around crops, then the first towns and cities, which eventually grew into empires. For the first time ownership of land, buildings, and surplus food appeared as part and parcel of human life. Animals, plants and tools were no longer part of the commons. No longer was food shared equally among all members of the group. The new way of living allowed people to specialize in a particular job or task and gave birth to a world of looking out for number one. Food surpluses created a powerful controlling elite with societal subclass hierarchies, from rich to poor. The social unit shifted from the tribe or the group, to the family. With separate families living in separate individual homes, each family tended to its own and its members' needs instead of the group as a whole, a model that exists to this day.

Our propensity for short-term thinking quickly got us into trouble. When a group of people settled in one area, constructed buildings, grew their food and expanded their population, the local resources became strained. Wood was needed for construction and fuel. Land had to be cleared for crops. A steady supply of fresh water needed to be available and methods of disposing human and animal waste had to be considered. Grazing pasture was needed for the domesticated animals. Other animals in the area were hunted more intensely, and plants used for clothing, medicine and food were inevitably over harvested and became more difficult to find. None of this was obvious at first. It takes a long time for these problems to present themselves, but the process is put in place the moment a human population stops wandering and settles down. Staying in one place created problems that we would be dealing with for the next ten thousand years.

When we clear a swath of land, strip it of whatever was growing there before and plant rows and rows of the same of plants while excluding all others, we create an artificial, unbalanced environment. Nature, left to her own devices, mixes things up. Many plants, animals and insects live next to one another naturally in symbiosis and balance developed over millennia. Agriculture presents an unnatural, manmade ecosystem, and—as we've seen—when you change one thing in a natural system you change everything. Humans have been dealing with the same problems since shortly after the development of agriculture and settled societies, albeit on a smaller scale. Though the scale of their environmental destruction was smaller from a global perspective, the results were no less devastating to the people living in those early societies.

From the moment that humans began settling and refining agriculture, it took a relatively small amount of time before things went south for some fledgling civilizations. Evidence in some areas of the Middle East implies that within one to two thousand years after people settled in that area they were forced to move on due to erosion brought on by deforestation and severe environmental degradation. The ancient Sumerians, one of the first advanced civilizations the world had seen, grew their society in the rich Fertile Crescent, considered the birthplace of agriculture. They became prosperous growing wheat and barley among other crops, but problems from deforestation, degradation of soil from overuse and over-salinization from irrigation arose within several hundred years. Growing populations put more pressure on the land and can eventually collapse a system completely.

Mesopotamia also grew large on the bounty of agricultural skills. The population, which approached one and a half million people, created more demand for greater agricultural production. New canals were dug to bring more water to the fields, resulting in over-salinization and waterlogged land, in turn leading to a dramatic drop in population and power.

For all the stories about opulence and riches, ancient Rome had its own problems with the environment from pollution, cooking fires, tanneries and craft workshops. Deforestation and over grazing led to the erosion of croplands. Erosion from the destruction of the local forests created runoff in streams and rivers that clogged up ports and estuaries. What was once fertile became unusable for agriculture, weakening the empire and contributing to its eventual collapse.

Ancient China ran into the same problems, as did Ethiopia. By 600 BCE ancient Greece showed alarming signs of over forestation, erosion and over grazing. A large amount of what was once rich cropland became unusable.

In the North American heartland, the Anasazi people, who were successful for a long time, converted great tracts of forested land into deserts through over harvesting for building materials and fuel, rendering their large population unsustainable and leading to their collapse.

The mysterious Mayan Empire in the jungles of Mexico and Central America left impressive monuments behind for us to ponder. The fact that the Mayans disappeared so suddenly has been the cause of much speculation. It is now generally accepted that their growing population, sustained by clearing patches of tropical forest for agriculture—coupled with a continuous state of warfare, which required large armies that had to be supported by even more agriculture—led to their collapse. In tropical rain forests most of the nutrients are stored not in the soil, but in the plants themselves. When forest is cleared for growing crops, it quickly loses viability and the farmers have to move on to another place, letting the original cropland recover for many years. Deforested areas of tropical rain forest are vulnerable to erosion as the topsoil layer is thin. After a point, Mayan agriculture was unable to keep ahead of these environmental problems and their society unraveled.

The inhabitants of Easter Island, the eastern-most island in Polynesia (so named because it was first discovered by Europeans on Easter day), have perhaps the most compelling story of all. Once a lush, forested island, its population turned it into a bare rock with hardly any vegetation. They left an impressive collection of stone carvings, which is all they're known for today. They actually cut down trees to use the logs to roll the massive stone statues into place, burning the rest for fuel. You can't help but wonder what the guy who cut the last tree on the island was thinking. Once home to a large population, by the time Europeans arrived Easter Island's population was down to a few dozen ragtag survivors.

There are hundreds of other examples of societies wreaking havoc on their environment. Air pollution, water pollution, erosion from clear cutting, degradation of soil and cropland; these problems are as old as recorded history. The only upside for some of these earlier societies (with the notable exception of the residents of Easter Island) was that after they rendered a place unlivable they could move to another place to begin again.

Why is it that despite thousands of years of bad examples from which to learn, we continue to repeat the same behaviors, getting the same results, and then acting surprised? It can be argued that the first agricultural societies could be forgiven for not realizing that what they were doing would lead to so many problems. After all, the Earth's bounty in their day must have seemed endless. The forests went on forever, the sky went all the way to heaven, and the fresh water just kept flowing. What could go wrong?

After endless repetitions of environmental disasters throughout history, it's time that we thought things through better. Long-term thinking is called for and it's needed now more than ever. Today, with our swollen population and the magnitude of our undertakings, when we mess things up it's becoming more and more difficult to recover. We won't be able to project our actions into the future until we develop a better understanding of time—deep time—which is the subject of our next chapter.

2

A ROAD TRIP THROUGH TIME

Those who cannot remember the
past are condemned to repeat it.

George Santayana

Adopt the pace of nature;
her secret is patience.

Ralph Waldo Emerson

A young person sees the world as a still
picture, immutable. An old person has
had his nose rubbed in changes and
more changes and still more changes
so many times that he knows it's a
moving picture, forever changing.

Lazarus Long, from *Time Enough For Love* by Robert A. Heinlein

It has been said that when humans first encountered the world of quantum mechanics, that mysterious through-the-looking-glass domain where the laws of physics refuse to follow the known Newtonian rules, it was the first time that we came across something we could see but that our brains were unable to fully comprehend. I would venture to say that the concept of deep time presents a similar challenge. We have great trouble getting our heads around it.

By deep time we are talking about time measured in millions or billions of years. In our modern world we throw these numbers around lightly. For many they've lost their meaning. We have become inured to them. We certainly can't imagine what a billion years really represents. As with quantum physics our brains aren't wired for time at that scale, but to get some idea of how long a billion years really is, consider this: A billion seconds ago it was 31.6 years ago. A billion minutes ago was just after Jesus was alive. A billion hours ago our ancestors were living in the Stone Age (presumably playing truth or dare). A billion days ago nobody walked the Earth on two feet.

We use the term "prehistoric" to mean before we kept written records or built things that we can see today, like the pyramids in Egypt. Beyond that, it's like wading into the sea. Our current lives occupy dry land. Then we wade ankle-deep into the recent past, then out up to our waists and chests into the ancient past. Soon we're standing on the edge of the continental shelf of our awareness of the past and everything slides down into the murky, unexplored depths of deep time, the before-time, the long, long ago. Why is it important to try to understand time scales of this magnitude?

Perspective.

There are benefits for those who gain perspective on nature's time scale and our place in it. Just as an older person, through life experience and a longer view, has greater wisdom and insight, so can we all gain wisdom and insight when we step back from our short-term perspectives and embrace the long term. Doing so helps us reprioritize what matters to us as individuals, to the planet and the future. Just as small children focus only on what is right in front of them, losing sight of the big picture, we too tend to focus only on our brief moment of time, losing perspective of the long-term ramifications of the decisions we make. If we make the effort collectively and as individuals to expand our perspective of time and our place in it, we will see that asking "what if?" before making decisions can help us avoid looking at the mess we've created and lamenting, as we so often do, "if only."

Earlier civilizations lacked the perspective we have today. They were trying things out, learning what does and does not work. We have the benefit of their mistakes. We can look back through our history and see exactly what not to do. For example, don't cut all the trees down, especially if you're stuck on an island. Don't pollute the river so badly that it bursts into flame, as we did several times with the Cuyahoga River in Ohio. Don't spray DDT to kill mosquitoes without thinking about what else you might be killing. Don't invade Russia in the winter. The lessons are there for us if we choose to use them, but we need a long-term perspective to apply them.

Scientists are in general agreement that the Earth is around four billion six hundred thousand years old. We have been around for about two million years, and in our modern form, genetically and behaviorally, for only about 50 thousand years. We stopped wandering around and started living in settled communities only about 12 to 15 thousand years ago. All of recorded history spans only about six thousand years. Taking the long-term view, we, as the song says, have only just begun. We are the new kids on the block.

In our anthropocentric viewpoint, we imagine that the planet is and has always been all about us and that we'll always be here. To us it seems as though we always have been here, but as Carl Sagan once said, "No species is guaranteed its tenure on this planet." The average species on Earth only lasts about four million years. That would put us currently about halfway through our run. A disconcerting fact is that 99.99 percent of the billions of species that have ever lived on this magical, life-friendly planet are now extinct. Let us not, in our arrogance and short-sightedness, suffer the illusion that our place at the table is guaranteed, or that Mother Nature cares if we disappear to make room for whatever comes next. It would behoove us to understand that our existence here is a precious, unlikely gift, one we need to actively nurture if we want it to continue. Today's environmental and social problems demand that we stand back and take a long-term view of our actions, or we will join the 99.99 percent of species that have come and gone before us.

To get a better grip on understanding the epic time scale in which nature does her work, we can explore the vast, temporal wilderness that lies outside our day-to-day understanding, and work together to gain a wider, wiser perspective of our planet, life and our place in time, and apply that new perspective to improving our lives and our planet.

There is an old episode of Rod Serling's television show *The Twilight Zone* in which the main character found himself accelerated to great speed, though it seemed normal to him. Because of his greater speed, to him the rest of the world appeared frozen in place, and because of his speed no one else could see him. Birds and airplanes appeared to be stopped in mid-air, people in mid-step; cars were frozen on the road. Things were moving, but so slowly it would take hours or days for him to discern the smallest motion in everything around him. He wandered through what appeared to be a fixed, static world. In reality it was a matter of different temporal perspectives.

With our short life spans and short history, we are like the man in *The Twilight Zone* when compared to the Earth. To us, the features of our planet appear fixed. Mount Everest stays really tall. The Grand Canyon remains grand and in one spot. The continents stay where they are. We know that Baja California, New Zealand, and the Falkland Islands will be there in the same place the next time we look. To us, things like mountains, islands and continents stay the same, but that perspective is an illusion. In reality everything changes radically over time; we just haven't had enough time in all of our history to perceive it with our own eyes. The reason everything appears unchanging is that this change happens on an incredibly slow and—to us—virtually invisible time scale. The continents, once joined in a super-continent, have over the past several million years slid to their present positions, and they're still moving. It is estimated that on average the continents move from about half an inch to just under four inches per year, a distance covered easily by a toddler's first step. It's easy to understand why it took so long for us to even conceive the idea that it was happening.

There is a large rock along the Sonoma County coastline in California called Goat Rock. When I go to the beach I can sit on the bluffs and watch the waves crash against it in a never-ending barrage. Goat rock sits there, seemingly impervious to the ocean's assault. If I go back and look at it again in 50 years I expect it would look much the same. But I am seeing merely a snapshot—one brief moment in deep time—of Goat Rock and its futile resistance to the ocean. Given enough time the ocean will wear it away, as it wears everything away that it encounters, and one day Goat Rock—like you and me—will be gone, as will the Rock of Gibraltar, Mount Everest and everything else we think is permanent.

Sonoma County also has redwood forests full of trees that live thousands of years. Walking through these age-old forests it occurs to me that our entire lives—birth, infancy, childhood, education, adulthood, parenting—all our passion, pain, drama, love, wonder, excitement and disappointments encompass nothing more than one breath in the life of a redwood forest. To ancient forests and rocks—to the Earth itself, which measures time not in years but in timelessness—our lives are but a flash of light appearing briefly before blinking out, like a Kansas firefly on a summer evening.

Every now and then nature provides us with more dramatic evidence that things are in flux, as when an earthquake knocks us flat or a volcano blows its top and changes the local topography. Occasionally we are blessed to witness the birth of a new island as an underwater volcano spews enough material from deep in the Earth to breech the surface of the ocean, reminding us that everything is transitory and that nature operates on a time scale that is almost unimaginable.

Some among us see the long term more easily than others. Ecologists, geologists, and other scientists who study nature's changes over time are better at grasping these time scales. When they look at a landscape they not only see what is in front of them, but past and future landscapes, what used to be there and where it's going.

My friend Rick Baker is a geologist and chemist and the Director of the Ocean Institute in Dana Point, California. His idea of a good time is to grab a small rock pick and a bag, put on a wide-brimmed hat and head out to the desert to poke around in the rocks he finds there. On sailing trips with Rick to Santa Catalina Island off the coast of Los Angeles, I would look at the coastline of California and see hills and houses. Rick would point out striations in the bluffs overlooking the ocean representing different geological epochs, the alluvial flows I hadn't noticed before and the differences in the types of rocks making up different parts of the coast. I can pick up any stone and Rick can tell me its history and approximate age, how it was formed and where. Looking at things through his eyes I could see that the world around me was rich in natural history and, rather than being fixed in one configuration, it constantly changed under the natural forces that came to bear on it every day. None of this is hidden. It is all there in plain sight if our eyes are trained to see it.

Another friend, Sonoma County Ecologist Tim Laughlin, also sees what others miss. On walks through the gently rolling hills near his home in Occidental, California, Tim's eyes dart about, missing nothing. When outside he's always picking off small leaves and plant parts to scrutinize them. Sitting with Tim on a hill overlooking a grove of trees, I see a lovely landscape without giving it much thought. Tim, however, can see that the trees we're admiring are of a species that moves in when old-growth trees have been cut. He sees a subtle drama unfolding. He can tell that the original, natural landscape has been disturbed and that there is a jockeying of position occurring among the various plant and tree species, each vying for dominance and balance as the landscape reinvents itself. He can tell me exactly which species will prevail over the next several hundred years, and what the view will look like at that time.

A ROAD TRIP THROUGH TIME

To understand deep time, join me for an imaginary trip through time. On this epic road trip, conceived and designed by Tim Laughlin, we'll travel from Homer, Alaska, across the great expanse of North America to the Empire State Building in Manhattan. This trip from Homer to Manhattan is about 4,600 road miles, dovetailing nicely, by adding some zeros, with the 4.6 billion years the Earth has existed.

On our trip through time, every mile we drive will represent a million years traveling at 60 miles per hour, which means that we'll be traveling one million years through time every 60 seconds. On this imaginary road trip we'll be using places in North America to represent particular moments in time. What follows was happening all over the globe; the trip represents time, not geography.

We start our journey in Homer, Alaska, nestled on the shore of Kachemak Bay. Homer represents the moment when the Earth first formed 4.6 billion years ago from the debris circling our young sun, after coalescing over millions of years into our home planet. At this point the Earth is a very inhospitable place, hot and lifeless.

First, we'll take Highway 1 northeast, then turn southeast on Highway 2, entering Canada at the small town of Beaver Creek, Canada's westernmost community. Nothing much happens for eight hundred miles, or eight hundred million years, then deep in the Yukon Territory, 3.8 billion years ago, we see the first evidence of single-celled life. That these organisms managed to find the spark of life from the messy ingredients provided is a miracle worth acknowledging. Forget the dinosaurs. Behold the original single-celled organism emerging from the primordial goop—ancestor to everything that has come after, including us. Infinitesimally tiny and invisible to our eyes had we been there to look for them, it took life a long time to ramp up to more exciting forms, but nature's rarely in a hurry. For a long, long, time, about two and a half billion years actually, these single-celled organisms were the supreme rulers of the Earth.

Continuing our journey, we travel another 400 miles—four hundred million years—to the Yukon/British Columbia border, where we find the first evidence of oxygen-producing bacteria, tiny life forms that began the long task of terra-forming our planet by filling the atmosphere with oxygen and making things nicer for the rest of us to come. It has taken well over a billion years to reach this point. We also see the first signs that those single-celled organisms are beginning to figure out that there is strength in numbers: they have begun organizing and forming into colonial organisms, the precursors to true multi-celled organisms.

Moving another billion and a half years, it's now 2.7 billion years since the Earth formed. We have traveled through half of Canada and arrived at the border of the United States at the town of International Falls. We are now in the late paleoproterozoic period, where we observe the first cells with true nuclei, a very exciting event in history, one that is necessary to make everything else possible in life.

We enter the United States on Highway 53 and head southeast to Duluth at the Wisconsin/Minnesota border. We rest here and have a celebratory picnic, for it is here, in the age known as the middle neoproterozoic after 3 ½ billion years, that we see our first evidence of true multi-celled organisms.

If cells hadn't figured out how to join forces, divvying up tasks among themselves and learning to specialize in one particular occupation while their fellow cells took care of their own jobs, all contributing to the whole, life could never have gotten any further than a murky soup of single-celled critters. It's a moment worth marking.

Our trip takes us through northern Indiana to the middle Cambrian era and on into Ohio west of Cleveland, where three hundred sixty million years ago we see the first vertebrates. This is when the first amphibians crawled out of the water, followed by the first reptiles. As we reach the Ohio/Pennsylvania border we see what is called the early carboniferous period, when the land becomes covered with large, primitive forests. Insects and other invertebrates show up to join the fun.

We have now traveled over 4.2 billion years through time and have arrived in Clarion County, Pennsylvania, 300 million years ago. Having traveled over 93 percent of our journey, dinosaurs finally appear, expanding their range to cover the planet. 80 miles and 80 million years later the first small mammals appear. Near the Pennsylvania/New Jersey border, 65 million years ago, the dinosaur's long run comes to an end and those tiny mammals grow and become dominant. Here is where the first primates appear.

The first hominids appear when we're well into New Jersey in the Middle Minocene era, over 95 percent of the way to our destination. Our genus, *Homo*, appears at the entrance to the Lincoln Tunnel near Newark, New Jersey, about two to two and a half million years ago. Going through the Lincoln

Tunnel and arriving in Manhattan on West 34th Street, just 200,000 thousand years ago, *Homo Sapiens*—that's us!—finally arrive, fashionably late. It takes us some time to evolve our culture and behavior to something approaching modern humans. We don't even learn to talk until 60,000 years ago, near the corner of West 33rd and 5th Avenue. There it is, the Empire State Building. We've nearly arrived! Let's get out of the car and walk from here. It's not far now.

We stop in the shadow of the Empire State Building to contemplate the fact that all of our recorded history—all those things we consider so incredibly old, like the ancient Mesopotamians, the Egyptians, ancient Greece and Rome—*everything*—encompasses about the last 27 feet of our journey to the front door of the Empire State Building.

My brother lives on a small sailboat that's nine feet longer than that. From Homer, Alaska, to Manhattan, across the entire North American continent, we have traveled 4.6 billion years through time, covering a *million years every mile*. On this scale our entire recorded history amounts to the length of two Volkswagen Beetles parked end to end.

Millions of species have come and gone before us and—if things pan out as they have in the past—lots more will follow. Life is truly tenuous. It didn't evolve with humanity as a goal. Evolution does not have a goal. Species evolve or die out from natural circumstances and natural selection. Like a stream running down a mountain, life follows the path of least resistance, supporting that which offers the best odds of passing genetic information on to the next generation. It doesn't play favorites and is indifferent toward the success of any particular species, including mankind.

So what are we to make of all this? Nature may be indifferent to our fate, but we certainly aren't. Of all the species that have ever lived on the Earth, we are the only one that has the capability to alter our environment so profoundly as to render it unlivable. We're also the only one that has the intelligence to make sure that our planet remains healthy and sustainable for life.

There is a growing awareness of the damage we have wrought, both in the environment and in our social institutions. We are increasingly aware of our environment's, and our own vulnerability. There is a lot of work to do, not only to repair whatever damage we have done, but also to change our way of thinking. Of the two, the latter may prove to be the bigger challenge. Our way of thinking is so entrenched, and everything in our world is so intertwined that to make real change in the way we live can seem too daunting to contemplate. It's like trying to roll a mountain away. There is so much weight and inertia that it seems impossible. The first challenge is to acknowledge the problem. That finally seems to be happening, albeit slowly. In the words of philosopher and social critic Ivan Illich, "What has changed is that our common sense has begun searching for a language to speak about the shadow our future throws."

Around the world there are thousands of grassroots nongovernmental organizations (NGOs) that have been formed, as environmentalist Paul Hawken put it, to restore grace, beauty and justice to the world. These organizations are elevating the consciousness of people in all walks of life by helping us to learn and remember. They are speaking out for minorities, clean rivers, safe food, fair opportunities, endangered animals, local economies, sustainability and justice. They are *not* speaking for corporate interests, for governments or those with narrow, profit-driven interests. You may be a member, or you may contribute money or time to one or more of these organizations. If so, you are on the leading edge of a social change in consciousness that is building momentum as you read this.

The Long Now Foundation, based in San Francisco, was established in 01996 to help us expand our long-term thinking skills by putting forth the core tenet that, for us to survive and thrive into the future, we must learn to think in the long term.

They use five-digit dates with an extra zero to solve the deca-millennium bug that will come into effect in about eight thousand years. According to their Web site one of their purposes is to provide a counterpoint to today's "faster/cheaper" mind set and promote "slower/better" thinking.

When The Long Now talks about long term they mean *really* long term. They hope to foster responsibility in the framework of the next 10,000 years, roughly the same amount of time that has passed since humans began using agriculture and developing modern technology. Their guidelines are simple: serve the long view (and the long viewer), foster responsibility, reward patience, mine mythic depth, ally with competition, take no sides and leverage longevity.

Author and environmentalist Stewart Brand, co-founder of the Long Now, says "Civilization is revving itself into a pathologically short attention span. The trend might be coming from the acceleration of technology, the short-horizon perspective of market-driven economics, the next-election perspective of democracies, or the distractions of personal multi-tasking. All are on the increase. Some sort of balancing corrective to the short-sightedness is needed—some mechanism or myth which encourages the long view and the taking of long-term responsibility, where 'long-term' is measured at least in centuries. Long Now proposes both a mechanism and a myth."

In 1997 The Long Now Foundation began work on an epic project. As an icon to their cause they began designing a clock intended to run for 10,000 years with little or no human intervention. Conceived by Long Now co-founder Danny Hillis, the clock will tick once a year, have a century hand that moves once every hundred years and a cuckoo that comes out every thousand years. An eight-foot high prototype of *The Clock of the Long Now* was completed in 1999 and is now in the Science museum in London.

Where do you put such a clock? No one city or civilization in history has lasted anywhere near 10,000 years. One can't assume that a society will be stable, capable or interested enough over that amount of time to sustain and protect the project. Natural catastrophes—earthquakes, tsunamis, floods and fires—happen with alarming regularity all over the world. Wars break out. Societies come and go.

The Long Now found what might be the perfect spot. They have purchased desert mountain land near Great Basin National Park in easternmost Nevada, land described as "a timeless landscape." They plan to install the clock inside the limestone cliffs on the west side of Snake Mountain at 10,000 feet elevation, in a landscape appropriately dotted with bristlecone pine trees, some of the oldest living organisms on Earth. They are preparing a site for a second 10,000-year clock in western Texas.

Visitors standing before such a clock will, presumably, be awestruck to find themselves in the presence of something intended to run for a period of time approaching four hundred human life spans. It may act as a sort of mild shock therapy to help us grasp time—past and future—beyond our ordinary awareness and help us understand that our lives are an infinitesimal part of something stunningly huge. It will teach us not to take ourselves so seriously, and perhaps rethink our priorities in the context of our new awareness. It will impart humbleness. As Stewart Brand said, "The trick is learning how to treat the last ten thousand years as if it were last week, and the next ten thousand as if it were next week. Such tricks confer advantages."

Some cultures and traditions have a better grasp of the long term. Buddhism encourages a very long-term view of the world and measures time in kalpas, a unit of time equaling approximately 16 million years. A "small" kalpa measures 1000 regular kalpas, about 16 billion years. This goes on up to a "great" kalpa, 1.28 trillion years, sometimes described this way: Imagine a huge mountain at the beginning of the kalpa, a mountain measuring

16 by 16 by 16 miles, much larger than Mount Everest. Take a soft cloth and wipe the top of the mountain once every 100 years. According to the Buddha, the mountain will be worn away before the kalpa ends.

Though it is where we live and all we know firsthand, the fact remains that there is nothing special about now. It is the current moment in an unbroken stream of time that cares nothing about the problems, mores, beliefs or inhabitants of any particular moment. People, aspen trees, mountains and fruit flies come and go. Time is just now, all the time.

Though people have trouble visualizing long periods of time in either direction, we find it easier to think about the past than the future. When talking about the past we have our history to reflect on. When pondering the future we fall into futuristic, silly images of Buck Rogers or the Jetsons, a world of flying cars (I still want one of those) and robots for maids, yet we often stand in awe when presented with artifacts from the past. Whether we're looking through a glass case at the objects that were in Lincoln's pockets at the time of his assassination, gazing at the Great Wall of China, holding relics from ancient Rome or a shard of pottery dating from the last ice age, if it's old we grow somber with the gravitas of physically connecting with the ages. People stand slack-jawed before Egyptian mummies or tools from the Stone Age found at some archeological site. We treat relics from the past with a respect bordering on the sacred. We take great care to protect and preserve these things, spending lots of money and using our best technology. We would do well to regard the future with the same sense of awe and respect. Time goes both ways.

We are part of the past *and* the future. Our sense of responsibility should project forward as well as backward. We don't have physical things from the future to hold and care for, but with a long perspective we can learn to treat our actions today with the same sense of fragileness with which we treat relics from the past.

Ironically, while we revere old things, we seem unaware that everywhere we go we are surrounded by ancient objects. Put this book down, go outside and pick up a rock and I can pretty much guarantee that it's infinitely older than anything you can find in an ancient history museum. That river near your home has been flowing for thousands of years; those hills in the distance were formed millions of years ago. The dirt beneath your feet has been here in one form or another since the formation of the Earth. Every living thing you see, from a butterfly to a giraffe to a hickory nut, represents the leading edge of billions of years of evolution. The bodies change but the life continues, leaping from generation to generation. The very atoms that make up your body have existed since the formation of the universe. Before they joined to form you, they spent billions of years as part of the vast cosmos of the universe—perhaps being transformed in the heart of an ancient star, light years away and long deceased—or as part of a swirling dust cloud circling another galaxy. Today those same atoms have mysteriously come together for a very short time to be part of you. Someday soon they will go on to be a part of something else. We are inextricably tied to the farthest reaches of the past and the future. Billions of years have passed and there are billions more to come. We are surrounded at every moment by the stuff of the ages.

3

DISTRACTIONS, DIVERSIONS AND THE FRANTIC PACE OF MODERN LIFE

The Gods confound the man who first
found out how to distinguish hours—
confound him too, who in this place
sets up a sundial to cut and hack my
days so wretchedly into small pieces.

Titus Maccius Plautus.

When I was in sixth grade my teacher tired of my antics and had me write this passage on the blackboard a hundred times: all time is irredeemable. The irony of doing this was not lost on me as I considered the exercise a great waste of time, though I never forgot the passage. Forty years later while researching this book I was surprised to come across it again in a T.S. Eliot poem called Burnt Norton. Here are the first few lines:

Time present and time past
Are both perhaps present in time future,
And time future contained in time past.
If all time is eternally present
All time is unredeemable.
What might have been is an abstraction
Remaining a perpetual possibility
Only in a world of speculation.
What might have been and what has been
Point to one end, which is always present.

Not having me read the poem to see where that bit of wisdom came from, my teacher missed a teachable moment and, as you may have noticed, she got it wrong. It's, all time is *un*-redeemable. In her defense, she was probably just trying to get me to shut up for awhile.

Reading that passage in context got me thinking about how we perceive time, not the deep time of the ages, but in our day-to-day lives and how it applies to the subject at hand.

Let's check in again with our truth-or-dare-playing caveman and cavewoman:

> *Cavewoman, hands on hips: "Where were you? You were supposed to be here* before. *The mastodon's cold."*
>
> *Caveman: "Well, I left* then *like you told me. I'm here* now."
>
> *Cavewoman: "But it's* after."

These blunt concepts of time, before, now, after, were all humans operated with for millions of years. Early humans lived within a framework of what is often referred to as natural time, or wild time. The natural cycles of the Earth, light to dark, season to season, youth to old age, were the temporal guideposts of their lives. Through millennia early people perceived time not as a series of events coming one after the other, but as cyclical. Life was measured in sunrises, sunsets, summers and winters, the movements of herds on their annual migrations, the coming and going of different plants—all of which existed in circles, great loops of life and death—that went round and round without end. Time wasn't something that started here and moved to there. Birth, youth, adulthood, and death came and went in repeatable patterns, like the tides and the movements of the stars.

For hundreds of thousands of years one generation's life was much like all that came before. Even if they possessed written language it would have been pointless for these preliterate societies to outline a chronological history of their lives and culture. For the most part, a history of all that came before them would be a very boring read—just an endless, repeating story of the same tribe doing the same thing in the same place, with different people. Sort of like your favorite TV soap opera. Early hunter-gatherer cultures, if they thought about it all, saw themselves as living in the middle of a great eternal now. Things cycled but didn't change. Everything came back to the beginning and the past and future coexisted, converging in the eternal now.

Time lived this way is not about moving on to something else, it's about returning; regeneration. You remain in the now as time circles around you. Cultures with this view of time don't see the past as dead and gone. For them, the past and future are always accessible in the now. This is sometimes referred to as "kairos" time, an ancient Greek word that describes time that is not measurable, but fluid and qualitative. A kairos perspective of time places you in the middle of things, where time comes at you with the dawn, travels around and past you while you go about your business and then passes into evening, only to come around again the next morning.

Our cleverness and inventiveness has changed all that. Modern societies see life through the lens of clock time, which, in the grand scheme of things is a new construct, only coming about in the last seven hundred or so years. Instead of seeing time as cyclical or fluid, in western culture we perceive time as a straight line, leading from all that happened in the past to all that will happen in the future. The Greek word for this type of measured time is "chronos," where we get the words chronology and chronicle. With this view time moves in one direction. Instead of seeing ourselves living in the now with time cycling around us, we perceive the world as static, while we move through it along time's path, always leaving the past behind and heading into the future. We see time as a one-way street.

We are so inundated in this sense of time that is driven into our consciousness from an early age that we think it's the *only* way to perceive time. When we learn about "primitive" cultures that see time differently, we think it's quaint or mildly interesting, but we rarely try to understand their viewpoint or consider another way to perceive time and our place in it. It is interesting though to observe how so many of us yearn to get away to places that are less obsessed with time, to escape the tyranny of the clock. I saw a man wearing a t-shirt that read, "Don't bother me, I'm on island time," a sentiment we can all understand.

Today most of us live as frenzied slaves of clock time. We over-schedule our children's activities and race from one thing to the other, always checking our progress against the clock and our appointment books. Here's a question: what's the very first thing you do when you wake up in the morning? Whatever your first answer was—go to the bathroom, make coffee—I would bet that the first thing you actually do when you open your eyes in the morning is look at the clock.

It's ironic that in cultures with few or no clocks, everyone seems to have lots of time on their hands. Almost magically, the less a culture measures time, the more time they seem to have. Conversely, the more we measure and dice up time into little fragments, the less time we perceive we have. Clocks and tight schedules, along with the myriad "time saving" devices we have invented, ("I'm not selling vacuum cleaners, Madam, I'm selling spare time!") create a climate where time is rushed, in short supply and always running out.

We cannot escape the trap we have created unless we effect a fundamental change in the way we perceive time. We have to realize that this harried, over-scheduled, frantic view of time literally exists only in our minds. As author Jay Griffiths said in her book *A Sideways Look at Time,* "There's hope in everyone if time can be seen as a—mere—construct. It's hard though because since childhood people are taught to see this construct, this edifice of time, as if it had a physical—concrete—quality... but wild time is still everywhere—our measurements of it are not made of concrete but of convention—and we could, if we wanted, huff and puff and blow the house of clock-time down."

The passage above underscores something that runs through many, if not most, human conventions. Much of what we perceive as irrefutable reality only exists in our minds. Together a society creates a set of beliefs supported by collective agreement. The way we perceive time is one of those agreements. *We*, not nature, are the ones who have carved up the day into 24 hours, and carved those hours into minutes and seconds. *We* are the ones who made up the seven-day week, with its hump day in the middle and the weekend that cubicle workers live for. "Thank God it's Friday," we say, but it's only Friday in our collective minds. To nature, it's just another spin of the planet. Even our calendar represents just one reality. The year 2000, which caused so much consternation and excitement around the world, was the year 1420 to the Muslims, 2544 in Buddhist time, and 5760 to the Jews. It's all a matter of what group reality you agree with.

Collective agreements are necessary for a society to function so we can get done what needs to be done. It's when we forget that these agreements are not fixed reality that we get into trouble by stressing about things that, when looked at with a long-term perspective, don't warrant that level of stress. Today's pace of change is faster than anything ever before experienced by humans. The effort to keep up with it is the cause of much pain and angst in our society. It may be time to check in with ourselves to see if our energy, stress, striving, and worrying is worth it—if it's getting us what we say we want in the long run. Many are finding that despite being surrounded by exciting new technology, entertainment, food, fashion and the latest and greatest of everything available, the answer is a resounding no.

We are predisposed to short-term thinking, which makes it even more difficult to question our mind-set of absolute immediacy in nearly everything we do. The "now," in our great-grandparent's day used to embody a season, or a period of several years. Now, the now is *right now*, this minute. Today people often think of the future in weeks or months, not years or decades. Our government operates largely within a 90-day window, looking for problems that will require attention within that short time span. Few government programs tackle the long view. The long view won't win votes.

Companies trying to bolster their quarterly reports come out with innovations so quickly and market them so aggressively that it creates the feeling of always playing catch-up. It's difficult to find a moment that isn't screaming *now! Right this second!* Our awareness is constantly focused on what is in front of our noses to the exclusion of the infinite time that spans around us. This shortens our attention spans to the point where, if we're not careful, we can lose awareness of the possibilities of a richer, deeper and more meaningful life. In her book, *Time's Pendulum,* Jo Ellen Barnett pointed out that, "To use a machine to divide time into minute portions was necessarily to shift humankind's focus of attention from eternity and toward the immediate things of the here and now." We can step back, slow down and regain our perspective. It is a choice.

None of this is to say that either living by wild time or clock time is superior. Both have their place, and clock time has enabled humanity to accomplish great things. We could not function as a society if we stopped coordinating our schedules and paying attention to the ever-present clock. Yet becoming too caught up in the minutia of what is going on right this second causes us to lose sight of the whole picture as though we're wearing blinders that obscure everything but what's right in front of us. We peer out into a small part of the reality that surrounds us, leaving little room for understanding of the deeper forces moving beneath our society and our lives.

Today's rapid pace of change and the rapid effects our decisions have on our lives and our world demand careful planning and consideration of the long term before we act, but learning to think long term will take practice. It's not something we're used to or encouraged to do. Our society doesn't offer many good examples of long-term thinkers. It celebrates instant successes and focuses on what is happening right this second. The long view asks us to understand and embrace the fact that sometimes it may be (brace yourself) better if something takes a little longer or costs a little more.

In our culture we expect things to happen fast. There are entire industries devoted to speeding things up. Companies constantly push their products or services with promises of "quicker" and "faster." We tap our fingers with impatience waiting for phone calls to connect, or computers to boot up. We want our food faster, our banking faster, our news faster, our travel faster and our lives faster. Time is money, we say. We treat slow with disdain. Saying someone is "slow" is to say they are mentally challenged and not up to par.

We often look with suspicion on those who just stand there, doing nothing. Cops come and ask them to *move along buddy, do something, go somewhere—speed up!* Our obsession with speed continues to shorten our attention spans and, as Paul Hawken put it, "…shorter attention spans are causing decisions to be made with quicker time horizons…which is making for a foreshortened and badly imagined future."

In Europe enough people decided that things had gotten out of hand with the frenetic pace of our world that they got together and formed The Society for the Deceleration of Time, a name which for me brings up visions of happy stoners on the beach. Their Web site explains that, "despite its name and the salutary amount of humor with which its members approach very serious matters, it is anything but a joke." They claim 700 members, mostly from Germany, Austria, and Switzerland. Their Web site declares that "...we have the impression that the wheel of history is turning at ever greater speed, that it is becoming more and more difficult to stand still for a moment and take a more contemplative view." Their declared aim is: "Every member should, regardless of what kind of activity he or she engages in, prolong the time taken for that activity whenever it makes sense to do so. They should stand up for the right to pause for reflection in situations where mindless activism and vested interests produce solutions which are expedient rather than genuine."

I could not agree more. We need to slow down and give ourselves the time our life decisions deserve. We would do well to revisit the maxim, "all in good time."

If a man or woman from fifty or sixty years ago managed to time travel to today, he or she would be less surprised by the technology and more surprised by cultural changes they would find, foremost among them the speed at which our society operates. A person from the forties or fifties would be overwhelmed by the amount of information thrown at them each moment. They probably thought they lived in a fast-paced world, but they had no idea what was coming down the pike. They didn't have cell phones, computers, voice mail, cable

TV or pagers. Back then, if the phone rang and nobody was home, nobody answered and the caller had to try again later. If they took a walk or went for a drive, nobody could get in touch with them.

Before email people held long, slow conversations by mail. Some of our most valuable national treasures are the thousands of letters written by great American leaders and thinkers who carried on epistolary relationships for years. Even chess games were played by mail over months, each player taking days to contemplate their next move before mailing it off to their opponent. That luxury of time was part of a world whose last days were rapidly approaching.

I remember my father explaining one day why he liked to play golf. "Whoever they are," he said as he pointed out to the greens, "they can't find you out there."

That's not true anymore. Every golfer's belt has a cell phone hanging from it. Today we're rarely unreachable. After the Second World War soldiers returning from overseas took weeks or months to make the trip by ship, giving them time to process their experience and get ready for home, to separate one experience from another and give both their due. But things were already beginning to speed up. Soldiers returning from Vietnam, by comparison, often found themselves walking the streets of San Diego within 24 hours of participating in a gun battle outside of Saigon. Today a soldier can be dodging bombs in Kabul one day and in Virginia the next.

The pace of change has affected all aspects of modern life. In nature, species can adapt to change when it comes slowly enough to provide time to move, or evolve. When it happens too fast, if they can't move or change in time, they die out. Our current pace of change outstrips our ability to adapt physically, emotionally, and culturally.

Our obsession with fast-paced life has caused us to focus on only the fleeting aspects of society: current events, fashion, and pop culture, ignoring other important aspects which operate on different time scales even though they exist side by side, simultaneously. Stewart Brand in *The Clock of the Long Now* observed "six significant levels of pace and size in the working structure of a robust and adaptable civilization. From fast to slow these levels are:

Fashion/Art/Pop Culture
Commerce
Infrastructure
Governance
Culture
Nature

In a healthy society each level is allowed to operate at its own pace, safely sustained by the slower levels below, and kept invigorated by the livelier levels above."

All of these levels are necessary for a stable society. The upper levels flash by at breakneck speed. This is where we try ideas out. Fashions—Nehru jackets, bell bottoms, shag haircuts, Earth Shoes—come and go. Fads—Beanie Babies, pet rocks, Hula Hoops, the Macarena—appear and disappear overnight.

The evening news focuses our attention on what they assure us is a very important story, and then dumps it instantly when something else arises.

Commerce tries to keep pace, but at a slower speed, following the trends and attempting to bring to market those products that will sell to the current mind set. Our infrastructure—the electric grid, roads, sewers, telephone networks and buildings—provides the hardware for all of this to happen. Changing the infrastructure is a difficult, expensive and slow process.

Our government changes players but remains largely the same over long periods of time. We complain about it, but we count on its stability and predictability. Changes in the way we govern ourselves are not usually made without serious debate about the ramifications the change will bring.

Our culture changes slower still. The stories we tell ourselves about who we are, our traditions, social mores and shared history provide a solid, long-term foundation upon which to build everything else. With our culture intact we feel free to try out new things, like a child climbing up the slide in the park, nervous, but knowing her parents are close by. The longer, deeper cultural time scale is important to our sense of stability. It's the most resistant to change and it's where we go when we're feeling vulnerable. We saw ourselves fall back into the comfort of our core culture after the attacks of September 11, 2001. Shaken, we all wanted to embrace our heritage and spend more time with family. It took awhile for us to open again to stupid celebrity news and pop culture. (The hilarious spoof newspaper The Onion reported in a headline after 9/11, "A Shattered Nation Longs To Care About Stupid Bullshit Again.")

After the Russian revolution the population referred to themselves as Soviet, but underneath the change in government their culture remained intact and the people quickly reverted to their Russianness after the communist experiment ended, as did all of the ethnic populations that had been absorbed into the Soviet system.

Slowest of all, changing over eons, the bedrock for everything else humans have done or will do, Mother Nature shows up every day, providing the raw materials of air, food and water that make it all possible.

Underneath our pop culture and flashy new technology lies the slow strength and power of nature's long-term reality. It brings down mountains, moves continents and always, always wins. We are like mites dancing on the back of an unimaginably huge beast, scarcely aware of its existence. It will lumber along on its own destiny while we live and die by the billions. Though it is difficult to affect the beast, when we do—by ignorance, greed or stupendously stupid short-term thinking—we would do well to understand that changing it back is next to impossible. A deep, reverent awareness of the underlying reality that is the true backdrop to our existence will provide us with the incentive and solemn commitment to act as though we are but a fleeting part of something much larger that demands our respect.

Problems always arise when we ignore the slower elements mentioned above or attempt to force them into faster timelines, like when for commercial purposes we harvest timber or fish faster than nature can replace them, or use rivers as dumping grounds for chemical factories, or allow our entire economy to be structured around cheap, plentiful oil while ignoring the fact that the long-term availability of oil is limited. When we only focus on the short term and believe that pop culture is our culture, we forget the adage that this, too, shall pass, and risk damaging or losing the slower, stable elements of our lives that we all depend upon.

Over the past 15 or so years our government has been tearing up 240 years of constitutional tradition, throwing out such rights as privacy, free speech, fair trials and the right not to be tortured, all for the sake of short-term expediency. This flagrant disregard for the constitution shook our self-image and rocked our nation as much as did the attacks of September 11. The debate rages to this day over balancing our core values with the passing needs of the moment. The lesson to take away is that a longer attention span and a longer point of view protect our environment, our culture, our government and our well-being.

The media have helped pave the road to shorter attention spans. We used to have more time to digest news. Newspapers, word of mouth and newscasts came on once or twice a day. We learned what was happening and had time to process it. With the proliferation of cable TV though, there are now dozens of competing news stations, each having to fill not 90 minutes or an hour in the evening, but every minute of every day. Because of the nature of the medium, radio and television cannot abide silence. A few moments of "dead air" causes listeners or viewers to push a button and tune to the next station almost immediately. Every second must be filled with chatter or attention-grabbing graphics or they risk losing their audience. They simply never shut up.

Because of the intense competition for our attention and the endless hours they must fill, news stations run fatuous, hollow stories filled with gossip and gratuitous titillation. We are regaled with stories about which celebrity left the house without underwear, or gained or lost weight, or who is dating whom. With so many vital issues facing humanity, we couch sex and celebrity as news. When the media doesn't have a story or has nothing to say, they make up false controversy or put stories out that are not really news. Anything to keep talking.

This climate of ever-increasing speed and change has been insidiously woven into the fabric of our society over the last century as air travel, television, cell phones and the internet became ubiquitous. Despite all the extra time these things were supposed to provide, Americans work longer hours than ever before and take less vacation time than workers in just about any other western country. Though it may not have been our intention, we have allowed our attention spans to shorten, our working hours to lengthen and our quality of life to diminish, compressing our view of time. Like the wanderer unable to see the forest for the trees, without gaining distance and perspective it's difficult to see what's going on while sitting in the middle of chaos.

There are millions of websites available at the touch of a button. Cable TV offers hundreds of programs and our cell phones offer up-to-the-minute news and information. Billboards scream messages at us while we listen to talk radio hosts hammering away at their agendas or spewing celebrity news. Sometimes it seems impossible to get away from the madness. Gas stations have even installed television screens on their pumps to market products and entertain you while you fill up your car. Images flash before our eyes at breakneck speed.

Our politicians communicate to us in five- or ten-second sound bites, appealing to our emotional hot buttons, knowing they don't have to offer in-depth analysis. They are counting on the fact that we won't pay attention long enough to process it, and they're usually right, rendering us vulnerable to manipulation by leaders and organizations with specific agendas. They are skilled at taking a well thought out, nuanced argument, and boiling it down to a talking point. By grabbing one hot-button issue, the populace often gets sidelined into becoming one-issue voters.

Abortion, gun control, flag burning, taxes, prayer in schools; leaders know that they can divert our attention with these issues, allowing them to slip other important things past our scrutiny. The media enables them. When our government is grappling with a large issue, the media will take any offhand remark and splay it across screens, endlessly repeating it, often out of context, inviting talking heads to comment on the comment. This constant attention on minutia diverts us from holding a real dialogue on the things that matter. Instead, we react to sound bites that have little or no depth or substance. It is not news; it is inflammatory rhetoric.

All of this is intended to engage our lowest common emotional triggers, allowing us to be manipulated with non-stop political and marketing messaging. Our elected officials often slap together badly conceived legislation to appease the moment, which then has to be overturned in the next election cycle. Many important bills are voted on without congressmen or senators reading them. Who has time to read legislation?

In our personal lives we often don't have the time to fully process one thing before we have several others in our lap. We are so distracted by the world around us that it precludes introspection and reflection. At work we typically only concentrate on one task for a matter of a couple minutes before we are distracted by phone calls, emails and instant messages popping up on our screens, co-workers stopping by, or other more urgent tasks that make us set aside whatever we were doing.

Even with the proliferation of junk mail, the United States Post Office loses billions of dollars a year because we no longer communicate by "snail mail." Most of us communicate by email and short text messages that don't lend themselves to reflective communication. Jokes race through the World Wide Web; cute photos are passed around from screen to screen. There is more communication among people than ever before in our history, with a concurrent lessening of substance. We have never been more in touch with each other with less to say.

Our young people have never known a slower world. They grew up in the midst of a chaotic blitz of media and marketing. Parents rarely send their kids out to play anymore. Fear and a desire to give them every advantage have caused parenting to become a montage of scheduled events for the children. Parents cram their own busy schedules with these extra tasks; driving their children to music lessons, organized sports, private tutors, classes, and my favorite, play dates. These have replaced the old-school parenting philosophy of kicking the kids out of the house and telling them to be back for dinner before the street lights come on. This over protective, over scheduled life precludes children having time to dream, imagine, and puzzle things out for themselves. They don't spend as much time lying in the grass watching the clouds, building forts or climbing trees. Instead their down-time activities revolve around videos, computers and video games. If an adult's not telling them what to do, they feel adrift. It's good for kids to be bored on long summer days. It provides the impetus for creativity.

Gone are the days of a group of boys playing an impromptu game of baseball in a sandlot using crummy old hand-me-down gloves and a torn square of cardboard for first base. Now virtually all children's sports activities are organized by adults, strictly bound by rules, and tightly scheduled. Children are growing up with no sense of deep time or the luxury of boredom. Many have never known the joy of an endless summer day stretching out ahead of them with absolutely nothing planned, a day of infinite possibility.

Today's children have come up with a new paradigm of social interaction to replace long summer days of bike riding and tree climbing: texting. Virtually all children from middle school on up now have cell phones with them all the time, and they send text messages to one another endlessly. A recent

New York Times article discussed the problems arising from the culture of text message communication. According to the Nielson Company, the average number of text messages sent and received by teenagers each month during the last quarter of 2008 was 2,272. This is the *average* number. Some do more. A reporter named Greg Hardesty in Lake Forest, California found that his daughter managed 14,528 text messages in one month. He wrote a story about it in *The Orange County Register*, which drove his daughter's monthly text messages to 24,000. According to the *New York Times*, when her grades fell, her parents confiscated her phone. They gave it back with a 5,000 text messages per month limit. How can anyone expect to get anything done with dozens of messages being sent or coming their way every hour? It's impossible.

In order to gain experience, assimilate information, and foster abstract, long-term thinking, we need time to ponder reflect, and compare. You can't do that when your phone is beeping every few seconds. A young woman I spoke to recently told me her friends commonly send messages saying things like, "What are you having for lunch?" or "This class is so boring." Like most teens she feels compelled to answer right away. There is a great desire in young people to keep their friend's approval and not feel out of the loop, even if the loop is annoying.

A recent newspaper article cited the case of parents who are suing the city of New York after their 15-year-old daughter fell into a manhole on Victory Boulevard on Staten Island. Why didn't she see the huge gaping hole? You guessed it; she was busy texting as she walked.

Many young people immerse themselves in online Internet games and cyber worlds. Some of these cyber worlds are quite detailed and rich in content, a whole other world in the computer. Young people create characters, or avatars, which become alter egos. They interact in these faux worlds with great passion, as though they were real. Some kids spend 15 hours a day doing this. This fake community seems to blind many young players to the real community around them. All of their attention and creativity is channeled into this made-up online world, while real, solvable problems swirl around them.

I once saw five adolescents gathered on a park bench, each of them holding a phone, carrying on a text-message conversation with other kids who weren't there. None of them were looking at each other or interacting with those around them. They seemed unaware that the others were there. Recently a friend of mine drove three teenage girls to the beach. During the drive the girls were almost completely silent, each with a phone in their hands, thumbs all punching letters on the little keyboards. It turned out that they were texting *each other* in the car, though they were sitting right next to each other.

But before we shake our heads at kids' incessant texting and immersion in the cyber world, we need to look at our own addiction to our Blackberries and email. We, too, have allowed these devices into our lives to the point where we think we can't exist without them. When Barack Obama won the presidency he fought tooth and nail to keep his Blackberry, which the secret service wanted to take from him for security reasons. He won. Most of us come home in the evenings and tune in to newscasts and other media. We check our emails, we read the paper, we surf the Web; we listen to the radio.

The daily news cycle is mostly a repeating litany of stories with little actual information. News stations advertise, "all the news you need!" or "up-to-the minute information!" The truth is you need very little of what they have to say, and you don't need it every minute. After being immersed in the constant white noise that is our media it can be disconcerting and wonderful to break away. The silence can be deafening, but in that silence are peace and an opportunity to decide what is important and what is not. Wisdom blossoms in the quiet places. After being away from the noise for a while, you wonder what all the fuss was about. The world of news and frantic information does just fine without you, and you can actually thrive without it.

When I was in my twenties, I worked as a crewmember on a 90-foot boat in Hawaii. We took tourists from Lahaina, on the island of Maui, to the islands of Molokai and Lanai and back again. At one point we had done several back-to-back trips, and for about two weeks I heard no radio, no television, and saw no newspapers. For two weeks I didn't pay attention to the clock or the calendar; I watched the sun rise and set. I watched whales cavorting in the channels between the islands and I forgot what day it was. What's more, it didn't matter what day it was.

For those two sweet weeks my sense of time felt separate from the frenetic pace of regular life. I was surprised at how quickly I slid into the rhythms of natural time and forgot about clocks. When we got back into port and I stepped back into the world, I was struck with how harried everything seemed, and this was in Maui! I overheard someone talking about the president being in the hospital, and I learned that President Reagan had by shot by John Hinckley several days before. I realized that for the first time in my life I had been so disconnected from the media that I'd missed a huge news story.

Out on the boat there was no way to learn of the news of the day. We had a two-way radio, but it was only for emergencies. As I acclimated again to the noise and pace of the world, I was not glad to be back. Music blared from cars. Headlines assailed me from every corner. I missed the peace and flow of life without clocks and distractions. I realized I had been given the gift of experiencing what life could be like when we step away from the madness.

Anyone who has gone to sea or spent long periods of time in the mountains or the desert away from the world has experienced that sense of calm that comes when the noise stops. It gives one a chance to take a breath and feel time moving at its own pace—natural time—and to cast one's vision wide enough to see the long view.

Wisdom and good long-term decision making require deep attention. When we are unable to take the time to think deeply into a subject, we cannot hope to understand its nuances or long-term ramifications. Distractions force us to jump from one subject to the next, never fully embracing either. We have to rethink our approach to decisions that affect our future. We cannot allow society's frantic pace to set the terms of our decision-making processes. It's time to slow down, step back and carefully vet our next moves, because our next moves will set the stage for all that follows. Let's explore some of the major considerations that must come to bear when we evaluate a decision with the long term in mind.

The first is sustainability. The best ideas, no matter how profitable, altruistic or wonderful they may be, are doomed to failure if the processes driving them are not sustainable over time. Long-term thinking and sustainability inexorably go hand in hand. In practice, however, the question of sustainability rarely comes up when making decisions. Elected officials rush into new policies and pass laws that temporarily please their constituents and earn them votes, or give momentary upper hand in some political situation. Often what they put into motion comes back to bite them, as when we trained and armed the Taliban to fight the Soviets in Afghanistan, only to find them years later using their training and weapons on us. We often question the sustainability of a situation only when we realize—too late—that it's not in fact sustainable.

Because of the worldwide Green Movement, sustainability is a concept that has gotten more attention lately. It's bandied about in all areas of the social and business spectrum, from corporate marketing to political activism. But what, exactly, does "sustainable" mean? Here is the best definition I've found.

Able to continue without lessening.

You'll want to remember this definition because we will be holding it up against all the subjects in this book. It's one you may find yourself holding up against decisions in your own life.

When the decisions we make are looked at through the filter of this simple phrase, it can be a real eye-opener. The disconcerting fact is that much of what we're doing in today's world is not sustainable.

The next consideration we need at the forefront when making decisions is this: how will what we're planning affect everything else? There is a desperate need for whole-system thinking in our world. Naturalist John Muir pointed out that, "When we try to pick out anything by itself, we find it hitched to everything else in the universe." The story of the Borneo Cat Drop from chapter one illustrated vividly how everything in the world is connected and if you change one thing, you cannot help but change something else. Thinking beyond the boundaries of the immediate situation is vital. Like good chess players, we have to do our best to think many moves ahead when altering any part of our environment, and create room for and ways to mitigate the inevitable cascade of collateral change that will occur.

Often we behave like the man in the fable who climbs a tree and begins sawing off the limb that he's sitting on. A passer-by calls up, "If you keep sawing that limb you're going to fall." The man in the tree ignores this and continues to saw until he cuts through the limb and falls with a crash, thinking, "That guy must have the gift of prophesy."

As you read this we are blithely sawing away at the limbs that support our entire culture and environment, and it doesn't take a prophet to tell us that if we keep it up we're going to come crashing down. Many of our "best" ideas have turned out to be huge problems in the long run. A little foresight would have helped offset much of what we face today.

A third consideration is to be sure that, when we're problem solving, we're actually solving the problem and not just hiding the symptoms. We often see the bad results we're getting but instead of trying to fix the root causes of the problems, which could cost more, take longer or require deeper thinking, we take the easier, short-term route and chase the symptoms instead. Television commercials show people suffering from indigestion from eating poorly, and then push antacids to relieve the symptoms, never for a moment suggesting that, I don't know, maybe less pizza is in order?

Insects are eating too many of our crops? Don't promote biological diversity. Douse them with pesticides. Dissatisfied with your life? Don't try to discover the cause of your dissatisfaction; buy this new car or this new gadget. Can't cope? Take this drug. It'll fix the symptom, at least for a while. Nearly all over-the-counter drugs treat symptoms instead of causes, but—as my sister used to say—you don't have a headache because of a lack of aspirin.

When I was a kid there used to be commercials for a detergent that was supposed to be great at cleaning men's shirt collars. These commercials showed distraught housewives upset and ashamed because their husband had "ring around the collar." They were happy to have this new detergent that would end their shame. When these commercials came on my mother would yell at the TV (really), "Hey lady, try telling your husband to wash his neck!" Now *that's* getting to the root of the problem.

Even if we couldn't predict the problems some of our decisions create, we can at least acknowledge that the problems do in fact exist, and begin to take measures to correct them. But we have gotten in so deep that fixing the problem can seem worse than ignoring it. The cure scares us more than the disease. Many of the worst problems we face today are so deeply intertwined in our economy that even the thought of changing them causes panic. We are so afraid of affecting the economy, losing jobs, changing the status quo or the balance of power, that we ignore something that will blow up in our face down the road in order to continue to benefit in the short run. We pretend it isn't happening and pass it on to the next administration or the next generation. In therapy they call this denial.

Denial has become necessary for us to get up in the morning and go about our business. If we were to face reality we would be forced to see that there are many, many things that demand our attention, things that are going to bite us badly when they reach the point where we can no longer deny them. For a long time we have been collectively sticking our fingers in our ears and singing, *la, la, la. . .*

In his excellent and funny book, *Farewell, My Subaru*, Doug Fine called this "the societal equivalent of not thinking about dying," but our way of doing things *is* dying, and denying it won't make it go away. The good news is that if we are willing to stand together and tackle these problems head-on, we can solve them. We have the intelligence, the know-how and the technology. We need to find the desire and the will.

4

CARS, SUBURBS, AND THE LOST ART OF COMMUNITY

It wasn't the Exxon Valdez captain's driving that caused the Alaskan oil spill. It was yours.

Greenpeace advertisement

New York Times, 25 February 1990

A healthy social life is found only, when in the mirror of each soul the whole community finds its reflection, and when in the whole community the virtue of each one is living

Rudolf Steiner

On September 12, 1899, a real estate agent named Henry H. Bliss was riding on a streetcar in New York City with his companion, Miss Lee. When the streetcar stopped at the corner of West Seventy-Fifth Street and Central Park West, Mr. Bliss got out and turned to help Miss Lee when he was struck by an automobile driven by Mr. Arthur Smith, which crushed his head and chest. He died the next morning, becoming the first recorded person in the Western Hemisphere to be killed by a car. The hapless driver, Mr. Smith, was arrested, charged with manslaughter and later acquitted by a jury that decided the accident was unintentional. In 1999 a plaque was dedicated at the site, "...to remember Mr. Bliss on the centennial of his untimely death and to promote safety on our streets and highways."

Like everyone else at the time, Mr. Bliss was ill prepared to deal with the new invention that had appeared without invitation on the streets of America. Noisy, ungainly and spewing noxious fumes, the automobile was considered by many to be a fad for the wealthy, a ridiculous and unwelcome contrivance that scared horses and confused people. When Mr. Bliss met his fate, cars were relatively rare. At the turn of the century there were only about 8,000 cars in the United States, but the rush was on. Within ten years of that first traffic fatality there were upwards of 250 automobile manufacturers nationwide, each turning out their own version of the automobile in small quantities.

For a while you could order a car through the mail from the Sears catalog along with your seeds and overalls. And though nobody bothered to record the second car fatality for posterity the numbers started to add up quickly. Within a quarter century cars were killing around 25,000 people a year, many of them children. Nevertheless, we all taught our kids to "look both ways," and over the next several decades we changed our homes, cities, and our lives to make room for cars, cars and more cars, until it seemed that cars, not humans, were the priority in our urban designs. And that's pretty much because they were.

Not long after the introduction of the Model T, movements arose to ban cars from city centers; but our exciting new love affair was too strong to regulate them so harshly, despite the toll they were beginning to take. We loved the freedom, affordability and status they brought. Like a cowboy riding off into the sunset on his horse, the car provided the perfect metaphor for the way Americans saw themselves: free, independent, and full of wanderlust. Modern cowboys could leave the horse in the barn. From then on when the horizon beckoned, it was the car that took us there.

Cars are arguably the most ubiquitous example of humanity's inability to predict long-term consequences. They fall solidly into our long, it-seemed-like-a-good-idea-at-the-time ledger. Who could have predicted back in the late nineteenth century, when tinkerers planet-wide were rushing to design the first prototypes of the new-fangled horseless carriages, that our new invention would change the landscape and the quality of our lives and our planet so profoundly? The invention of the automobile changed everything, everywhere.

It's easy to understand why cars seemed like such a great invention. They gave us freedom, opened up vistas not available before and gas was cheap and plentiful. What could go wrong? A lot, as it turns out. It's amazing that we continue to embrace autos to this day considering that they have done more damage, created more problems and killed more people than anything else we've ever come up with. To accommodate cars we have:

Turned many of our city and suburban landscapes into ugly, nightmarish scenes with the blight of broken-down cars, crumbly roads, and incessant traffic.

Paved millions of miles of arable land, rending it unusable for anything else, making it impermeable to rainfall so that water runs off without restoring the water tables on which we rely.

Redesigned our cities and communities in a way that makes them friendly for cars and unfriendly for humans.

Created a sub-class of citizens who cannot afford or operate a car, limiting their ability to get around and function. If you're walking or taking the bus instead of driving in our culture you're considered poor. Pedestrian is almost a dirty word.

Killed more people on our roads than all the deaths in all the wars we have fought.

Become dependent on countries whose people and governments hate and threaten us even as we send them billions of dollars every day.

Created billions of tons of tossed-away car parts and tires each year that fill our dumps and mess up our yards, roads and lives.

Sacrificed the lives of our sons and daughters in wars intended to secure our oil supply.

Spent billions on military operations to patrol and maintain our oil supply lines.

Killed a million or so wild animals every week, including deer, birds, squirrels, as well as our pets. Who among us hasn't run over an animal?

Created unprecedented pollution throughout our cities and the world, with a concurrent increase in health problems.

With all of the trouble they cause I'm surprised anyone gets near cars. If another country or a terrorist group were accused of doing the damage cars have done we would declare war, mobilize our nation's resources to defeat them and build memorials for the victims. Instead, we keep driving, eagerly anticipating each year's new models, and bury ourselves in debt to get a new car whenever we can.

It's interesting to note that in the beginning many considered the automobile a cleaner, more environmentally friendly mode of transportation, eclipsing the horses and the inevitable horse poop that crowded and dirtied our cities at the time. Cars today are so much a part of our lives that we seldom question them, but at one point or another I think we've all stopped for a moment to wonder at how crazy our car culture is. I know I have.

When I was about 16 years old, growing up south of Los Angeles, I found myself one day standing on a rise overlooking Interstate 5, a freeway that runs the length of California. It was rush hour, and I stood and watched a mind-boggling river of vehicles as they crawled along, trying to navigate the confusing interchanges. It was a hot California day and the heat shimmered off the blacktop. The smell of exhaust and oil permeated every breath. The sound of all those internal combustion engines combined into a numbing din, a sound that is as much the backdrop in many areas of Southern California as the sound of songbirds is in the trees in less congested places.

Nearly every car carried only one person. These were the large inefficient cars of the 1970s. Each spewed exhaust, some visible, some not. Their cumulative effect hung in the sky, casting a dull, gray veneer over everything. The freeway stretched off to the horizon in both directions, bounded on each side by closely-built stucco homes and dingy businesses, many of them mere feet from the freeway and sheltered by small, ineffective sound walls, their paint stained from the ever-present oil and exhaust in the air. Dirty, stunted plants clung to life along the edges of the road. It was all so dismayingly ugly and grimy. As I stood watching I had a minor epiphany and saw the scene as though for the first time, despite the fact that I grew up surrounded by landscapes just like this one. I saw it as a visitor from another planet might and a simple thought rose, unbidden, in my mind: *I don't think we can keep this up for long.*

So far we've kept it up for over a hundred years. Henry Ford came up with a way to mass produce cars by perfecting the assembly line, putting most of the other 250 car manufacturers out of business. Then in 1908 Ford introduced the Model T (also known as the Tin Lizzie), billed as the first affordable car. It cost $825 in 1908, but only $345 eight years later, due to the money saving assembly line techniques used by Mr. Ford. (Despite popular belief, the first automobile assembly line was not invented by Henry Ford but by Ransome Eli Olds, the creator of the Oldsmobile. Henry Ford improved it and turned it into what we know today.)

By the early 1920s there were 10 million cars in the U.S. With more and more cars appearing everywhere, we began creating the infrastructure to support them, which set off a century of transforming our world around the car. The way we live, work, do businesses, wage war, design our cities, eat and think were all changed irrevocably by the invention of the automobile. Virtually no place on Earth has been unaffected by cars. Anywhere you go, from sub-Saharan Africa to the arctic, to remote islands in the Pacific, you can expect to see some sort of car or truck rolling along.

It's hard to imagine that just over a century ago there were few cars anywhere. Horse-drawn wagons and plain walking were still in vogue. We had railroads that crossed the continent, streetcars and rudimentary bicycles; but until cars, people traveled at the same pace we had traveled for thousands of years—slowly.

Nobody imagined that in the near future cars would dominate the world, although in the earliest days of cars many people wanted to see the new invention take off in a big way. These were the people who happened to own and control much of the oil upon which the car depended. But let's back up a little.

In the 18th century the first prototypes of steam engines appeared. Powered by steam heated with coal, these early engines transformed the way we did much of the work that had been powered by humans or animals. In the 19th century the industrial revolution, sometimes referred to as humanity's second great transformation (the invention of agriculture being the first), gained a full head of steam, so to speak, and we never looked back. This was when we first started in earnest to burn the fossil fuels that had lain underground for millions of years. By releasing their stored energy we began the process of transforming not only our lives, but also our planet and our climate.

Up to that point we used animals or people for labor, and wood for our fuel. Everything from well pumps to factory looms to sawmills were transformed by the new steam engines, reducing the number of workers and animals needed while saving lots of money for the owners and upping their output.

At first coal mainly supplied the heat to generate the steam that drove the new machines. Like locomotives, some of the first automobiles were steam powered (imagine *that* chugging down the street). Then in 1859, in the farm country of Northwestern Pennsylvania, a man named Edwin Drake noticed that oil was seeping out of the ground in the area. He put together a team of financial backers and a chemist, and drilled the first oil well in a small town called Titusville. At that point there were no cars. Drake and his team were interested in oil as a possible commercial illuminant. After drilling just over 69 feet they struck oil and the Pennsylvania Rock Oil Company was formed, later renamed Seneca Oil Company. This was not the first time oil had been struck in the area. Many before Drake had struck oil while drilling for water, but they considered the oil a huge nuisance. Drake was the first to drill for oil on purpose.

Chemists analyzing petroleum discovered that it could be distilled into a variety of useful compounds, including an illuminant, lubricants and gasoline. On the heels of perfecting the methods to create gasoline, the internal combustion engine came puttering along, with its insatiable appetite for that very fuel. It created an entirely new, potentially huge market for those who controlled the oil. But even after the invention of cars, so few were being sold that gasoline wasn't yet a must-have commodity.

By the early 20th century most major cities had efficient electric streetcar or light rail systems. People were forgoing horses in great numbers and using public transportation to get around. Los Angeles, California once had one of the best public transportation systems in the world. It was affordable, efficient and served the needs of the population quite nicely. Today Los Angeles might be the worst major U.S. city when it comes to public transportation. L.A. freeways and traffic jams are the stuff of legend. What happened to its once great public rail system? One might suppose it got financially out-competed by people choosing to buy and drive cars instead of riding the train, opting for the greater flexibility of travel that cars offered over fixed rail lines. If we didn't want to ride the public rail lines we were free to purchase a car.

More people began driving cars and ridership on public transportation declined. This was exacerbated by the fact that the extra roads that were being built to accommodate the cars created more traffic and clogged downtown areas, making public transportation slower and less reliable.

In L.A. and in nearly half a hundred other American cities however, our "decision" to forgo public transportation for the automobile had more than a little help from people and corporations who had a vested interest in getting more gasoline powered buses and cars on the roads.

We were so enamored with our new mode of transportation that, as populations grew and the need for better transportation arose, most cities opted for widening roads over improving or expanding public railway systems. Detroit—Motor City—faced with this problem in the 1920s, went for bigger, wider roads instead of building a new subway system. Prices for public transportation rose and ridership declined. There were elements of these changes being driven by car lovers themselves, but some felt that the increase in driving and the concurrent decline in the use of public transportation shouldn't be left to the vagaries of the market.

In the 1930s a new company—National City Lines—was formed. Jointly owned by Standard Oil, General Motors and Firestone Tire Company, the company purchased public rail systems throughout the country and then proceeded to dismantle them. That's right, the company was formed with the express purpose of buying up and destroying existing electric rail systems serving millions throughout the United States. Over two decades in nearly fifty cities nationwide, over a hundred public passenger rail systems were bought and thousands of miles of track were torn from the ground, leaving passengers little choice but to ride the buses manufactured by General Motors or buy their own car, which would require buying oil and tires regularly.

So here we are. From several thousand cars a century or so ago, today there are around 270 million cars in the United States, and approximately 600 million worldwide. Those numbers represent just passenger cars, not buses, trucks and other commercial vehicles. As of 2002 there were over 117,000 gas stations in the United States. As our population grew, women left their traditional homemaker roles and joined the workforce and car companies marketed incessantly. More and more cars joined others on the already crowded streets of America. While car commercials always show new cars zipping down open roads in beautiful landscapes—their drivers unfettered and free—in reality most drivers navigate heavy, difficult traffic much of the time. The truth is that today many of our roads and cities are choked with automobiles.

As in Detroit, over the years the most common response to the growing number of cars in cities across the nation has been to build more and bigger roads. Ironically, it has been proven that adding more roads, or widening roads in dense traffic areas, does not ease traffic problems; in fact it increases them. The more roads you add, the more cars clog them. It's a catch-22.

In the mid 20th century the federal government began work on the interstate highway system, linking everyone from coast to coast. Though its ostensible purpose was to provide a way to quickly move our military from one side of the country to the other in an emergency, the interstate system was the final puzzle piece in our ultimate dependence on the internal combustion engine.

Cars became the reality around which we designed everything else for the infrastructure of our towns and cities. Zoning laws were passed requiring new businesses to provide ample parking, forcing buildings to be set back from the streets and large tracts of land to be paved over. I remember back in the 60s marveling at the fact that Disneyland, in Anaheim, California, had provided 100 acres of parking lot for visitors. At the time this seemed to me to be a great, modern achievement.

I find it endlessly fascinating that humans launch themselves into endeavors that we know can't be kept up over the long run. The big carmakers have always had just one goal: sell as many cars as possible for the highest price. Blinded by our love for cars and unable to imagine a world without them, we continue to construct more infrastructure for them—more roads, more parking lots, more pavement, more everything. Cars and trucks have become so much a part of life that by 1997 six of the ten largest industrial corporations in the world were car manufacturers or oil companies. Approximately one out of six U.S. workers make their living, directly or indirectly, from cars. They include the toll booth attendant, the guy at the gas station, auto parts stores, road workers, auto designers, auto body shops, loan officers, insurance salesmen, mechanics, car washes, taxi drivers, delivery men and drive-through businesses of all kinds. The list could go on forever. Cars got bigger, the gadgets in them got better, and the prices climbed and climbed.

If somebody were to step back at any point and ask if this is sustainable, the answer would have to be no. Would a rational person think that we could continue to endlessly put more cars on more roads forever and ever? What about when the resources ran out? The steel? The oil? The land? We never asked those questions, because the answers were too scary. How could we possibly turn back the behemoth we had created? Here is the model around which we've planned pretty much everything when it comes to cars:

1. Expect endless growth of the car industry.
2. Put millions of new cars on the roads each year.
3. Do this forever.

Gridlock, a word that first appeared in popular usage in 1980 during the New York City transit strike, has become a common term. For many the daily commute has become a daily nightmare, as we inch along our "free"ways in unbroken chains of exhaust-soaked shared misery. Twice each day millions of cars, almost all containing just one person, crawl out onto our roads, inefficiently moving millions of tons of steel and untold multitudes of sad-eyed workers to and from home and workplace. For some, the commute takes a greater toll on their well-being and their spirit than their work does. In many places what was once called rush hour has expanded to encompass most of the day.

Car manufacturers have attempted to mitigate this awful reality by making the interior of our cars as plush and luxurious as possible, with heated seats, cup holders, air conditioning and high-tech stereo systems. Lexus ran an advertisement that said, "You're an hour from work. You can't change your job. You *can* change your space," a direct appeal to those who feel trapped in their commute, and another example of trying to mask the symptom instead of actually fixing the problem.

In her book, *Asphalt Nation,* Jane Holtz Kay wrote: "The average car buyer must spend half a year's salary for an automobile. Over the long haul a "twenty-something" entering the workforce will spend four years of his or her life behind the wheel driving to the office. Like it or not, every family is in the transportation business, expending $9,000 to $11,000 in internal and external costs a year to drive each of their one, two, or three cars an average of ten to twelve thousand miles apiece."

I need to take a moment here and say that, like most Americans, I love cars. I really do. If you ignore the deaths, the smog, the cost of gas, insurance, and maintenance, the national vulnerability our dependence on oil brings, the blight of our traffic-clogged roads and the overall damage and cost to the environment—which is what is pretty much what we all do—well, they're just great, aren't they? I love taking drives along the coast with the top down. I love the freedom cars provide. I used to sell cars. There's really nothing like that exciting moment when a person first slides behind the wheel of a new car, all smiles and anticipation with a nose full of new car smell and visions of the open road, before driving off into stop-and-go traffic with an instant 25 percent or so drop in the value of their new car the moment the wheels leave the lot. It's a heady moment, one I've enjoyed as both a buyer and a seller.

Besides the problems stated above, our intense use of cars has created another, more insidious reality, one that has sort of snuck up on us. I'm talking about the creeping loss of a sense of community that we have experienced over the last hundred years. Cars have helped cause this in a couple of ways. First, they have served to isolate us from one another. There's something about climbing into a car and shutting the door on our personal steel and glass cage that makes us feel cut off from others, even though we may be sitting in a traffic jam with ten thousand others around us in their own personal steel and glass cages.

People do things while driving that they would probably not do when walking among others. Need I mention here the nose-picking driver? When we drive, it's like we're at home in our car. And we protect our homes, don't we? Behind the wheel drivers can get testy when they feel their space is being encroached upon. Road rage, another modern term, has become chronic in places like Los Angeles, where the daily stress from commuting in stop-and-go traffic has frayed drivers' nerves to the point of pulling guns out from under the seat and transforming the freeway into the O.K. Corral.

Why would a person who can normally control their impulses suddenly turn into a raging demon behind the wheel? I believe it's because since we feel isolated in our cars with our climate control and personal entertainment systems, the normal social conventions of politeness and courtesy don't apply anymore. That isolation, coupled with the stress of traffic and the fact that our cars are very expensive to repair, changes the rules.

It's amazing and scary to watch someone I know as a "nice" person get behind the wheel of a car and start yelling and cussing at someone who committed some driving infraction. I know a woman who, if you spent time with her, you would think was as sweet as a person could be, but from the passenger seat of her Jeep I watched that same woman race up alongside another driver to scream and swear at them, then spit out the window at the other car. The other driver's crime? He had changed lanes in front of her and she thought he didn't give her enough room, so she had to brake. I could only hang on, watch the show and think, *holy shit! Who are* you and what have you done with my friend?

Thinking about this, it occurred to me that in the grocery store if someone accidently cuts someone else off or bumps them with their grocery cart, rarely does the damaged party start screaming, "Hey, asshole! Watch where you're going!" or "Where'd you learn to shop!" while giving the finger and racing ahead of the other shopper to stop suddenly and cut them off in the aisle. Why? Because when we're face to face with others it's harder to be a jerk. It's the same way we can more easily fight a war if we demonize and dehumanize the enemy. If we have to actually meet them and get to know them, it's much harder to justify shooting them.

Walking down the street, people accidentally get in each other's way. The typical response is to excuse ourselves and go around them. Going in or out of a door we encounter others going the other way. Usually we hold the door open for them and step aside to let them pass, or they do that for us, but in a car if someone cuts us off or doesn't see us and gets in our way, it's okay to flip off the other person, shake our fists and scream epithets.

I heard a comedian recently tell the story of having an old lady cut him off while driving. "Hey, watch it you stupid old bitch!" he yelled, only to race up alongside her honking his horn and shaking his fist and suddenly realize it was his sweet, kindly old neighbor, Mrs. Bailey—a widow who knew his mother and used to bake him cookies—at which point he felt like an ass. And that's the point. Outside of a car he would *never* yell something like that at an old lady, no matter what she did. The culture of cars has blurred the lines of courtesy, shortened our tolerance for each other and precluded the practice of giving one another the benefit of the doubt.

I am happy to report that it has been at least 25 years since I've had any sort of angry altercation on the road. Why? Because I discovered the two magic rules of hassle-free driving.

JIM BRUMM'S MAGIC RULES FOR HASSLE-FREE DRIVING:

Let everyone do whatever they want to do.
Forgive everyone immediately no matter
what they do.

If you have a lot of trouble with other drivers, you might want to write those two rules down and tape them to your dashboard, because they work. Even if you're not one to yell and cuss at other drivers—and I realize that most of us aren't—cars still serve as personal iso-bubbles in which we navigate our world, insulated from others and cut off from direct interaction with those around us.

While those riding public transportation may not become fast friends with their fellow riders, there is still a sense of common purpose, a sense of community. A friend who is from England tells me that riders on buses and trains spend each morning and afternoon commute with the same people, sometimes for twenty or more years. Each day, she says, the passengers acknowledge their fellow commuters with a polite nod, but not much more. If the train breaks down and they're stuck for a while, those riders will strike up friendly conversations during the wait, only to revert back to polite nodding the next day. Even that mutual acknowledging nod however, though it doesn't exactly denote friendship, does underscore community and common purpose.

Life is different when you're interacting directly with others rather than being sealed off from them. You see their faces and you want them to treat you well, so you treat them well. On the street, the train or the bus it's just not as easy to be a raging jerk to people's faces. Cars have created a society with little opportunity for direct interaction in our travels. Mostly we try not to hit each other as we get where we're going, where we compete for parking spots. (When it comes to drivers fighting over "stolen" parking spots, refer to Jim Brumm's Magic Rules for Hassle-Free Driving.)

Speaking of those thousands of drivers commuting and turning the freeways into slow-moving parking lots each day, you have to wonder: where are all those people in all those cars coming from? Why do so many people travel such long distances to get to work each day? Why have we set things up so that for many of us our homes and our workplaces are so distant from each other, forcing long, expensive travel back and forth?

That brings us to the second way cars have helped us lose our sense of community. The invention of the automobile and the freedom of travel it offered paved the way for the creation of that modern wonder, the suburb, and the concurrent degrading of our cities.

At the beginning of the 20th century most people in America lived and worked in rural communities that were often sparsely populated and unattached to the cities. Small towns had their own economies with businesses not necessarily dependent on large cities for their day-to-day commerce. A lot more people farmed in those days, supplying food for the cities, but transportation was more difficult and sporadic so most farmers didn't transport their harvest over great distances like they do today. Today, only about 20 percent of the population lives in rural areas, with the rest packed into urban centers or the suburbs, often densely populated themselves.

Though the city centers were crowded and often had poor living conditions, they provided a deep sense of community. Sectioned as they were in the early days into Italian,

Jewish, black, or German areas, cities offered dwellers deep connections and roots to their local part of the city, with religion, ethnic customs and language binding them. Peoples' homes and work places were close together. They shopped at the local stores where they knew the proprietors. They knew their neighbors. Some inner-city residents rarely left their little corner of the city, living, working and dying in the same few square blocks.

As the country grew and people became more prosperous, some began to cast their eyes outward. The first horse-drawn rail lines, followed by steam and electric railways, allowed people to move away from crowded city centers and build or buy homes just outside the city. Smaller communities, closely tied to the larger nearby city, sprang up across the nation. At first, access to the railway station would be the plan around which housing and businesses would be built, but the advent of the car meant people were no longer tied to public transportation, so communities could be built farther and farther from the cities. Large highways were built to accommodate this new model.

Developers bought up hundreds of acres of outlying farmland and built hundreds of "tract" homes with a handful of design variations to sell off to city dwellers, who wanted to spread out. When those sold, the developers bought the next hunk of land and did it again and again, until the suburban sprawl covered thousands of square miles around our cities.

Early on suburbs were billed as offering "country living without the mud." They were spacious, bucolic settings away from the teeming crowds of the city. This plan not only destroyed a lot of good farmland, it put millions of suburban dwellers miles away from their places of work, requiring huge energy outlays to get them back and forth and creating a permanent need to own and maintain a car.

These new suburban homes were built with garages to accommodate the "two cars in every driveway" model that had taken hold. Planners thought not in terms of community or people-friendly environments, but in terms of cars. The question was not: how can we build a beautiful community that provides a haven and closeness for people? Instead, the questions became: What design will best accommodate cars? How can we make room for more cars? How can we make sure there are enough parking spaces? How can we make sure traffic keeps moving?

As the suburbs grew and evolved over time, a new model for serving suburban residents came into its own, the strip mall. Thousands sprang up in suburban areas all over the nation. Often garish and unsightly, these low-slung, single-story stores were built with huge parking lots along with ugly, obtrusive signage looming over the landscape, designed to be easily seen from a distance by drivers. Planners designed traffic patterns to get cars into these stores, not pedestrians. Today's suburbs often have wide and busy streets flanked on both sides by miles of strip malls. If you are on foot you have a problem; in fact sometimes you *are* the problem. Crossing these wide avenues is difficult at best and dangerous at worst. Stores are spread out over very large areas. The supermarket may be miles from the hardware store with the dry cleaners on the other side of town, requiring more driving and more gas burning.

In modern civic planning it is assumed that everyone has a car, and that everyone wants the most convenience for driving. One small community, 50 miles north of San Francisco, built hundreds of homes on one side of Highway 29, a busy, fast-moving thoroughfare that runs through the center of town. They built a new strip mall on the other side of the highway, with a supermarket, the mandatory Starbucks coffee shop, and a couple of fast-food joints. The trouble is that there isn't a crosswalk for pedestrians to get across this busy highway. There is a traffic light, but no crosswalk. Did the planners even consider this? So much for the neighborhood kids getting on their bikes and heading to the store for candy, or being able to walk anywhere. You might as well tell them to go play on the freeway. In that community, if you don't have a car you can't get around without taking your life in your hands. If you want a carton of milk you have to take the car, no matter how close to the store you are. Walking is out of the question. A quart of gas for a quart of milk is a bad tradeoff. And this is not an anomaly. Though some are better than others, suburbs all across the country were designed to accommodate our obsession and dependence on cars.

If you turn off the main roads in the suburbs, leaving the strip malls behind, you'll find where the customers of the strip malls live. Many modern suburbs consist of housing tracts, with perhaps five design layouts to choose from. Developers typically use two or three innocuous colors—light blues and grays perhaps—to break things up. Most of the homes look the same with just minor variations on the theme. Each home has a large lawn and a large driveway and garage. You'll find an SUV, a minivan or some other vehicle parked in many of the driveways. But here's the remarkable thing: if you drive through these neighborhoods, you'll often find most of the garages closed, and a remarkable dearth of people on the streets. Where is everyone? If they're not in commute traffic, fighting their way to or from work, they're locked up inside their homes. The green, well-tended front lawns sit unused and unenjoyed. The streets are quiet. Often you won't even see children playing. It's as though everybody got sucked up into the Mother Ship.

With all of these homes and people living in close proximity, and all the money and energy it takes to make it happen, in the end it comes down to lots of expensive, nice things but little sense of community. Compare this to the old inner cities of the past. Close-knit brownstones filled with people, children playing in the streets, people sitting on their stoops. Mothers sent their children down to the butcher or the baker to pick up something for dinner. The butcher or baker knew all the neighborhood kids and perhaps ran an informal line of credit to the family. This was true as well in old small-town America, where there was a deep sense of belonging and a feeling that you had a responsibility to your neighbors and community at large.

This is the "modern" model we used to construct our neighborhoods, market our goods and services and live our lives, but in the words of James Howard Kunstler, "(modernism)…

created a crisis of human habitat; cities ruined by corporate gigantism...public housing and public spaces unworthy of human affection, vast, sprawling suburbs that lack any sense of community, housing that the un-rich cannot afford to live in, a slavish obeisance to the needs of automobiles and their dependent industries at the expense of human needs, and a gathering ecological calamity that we have only begun to measure."

The trouble with so many modern suburban developments is that there is no "there" there. Often there is no defined city center, no sense of neighborhood and no place where people naturally congregate and visit. The design doesn't lend itself to these things. People may buy a home in this or that town, but it's often only because that's where they can afford to buy, not because of a particular specialness—unless it's the proximity to the freeway and the daily commute. Surveys have shown that the majority of homeowners in the United States cannot name more than one or two neighbors, though they may live near them for years. People in the suburbs often don't develop strong attachments to their towns; turnover in some areas is high as people continually search for bigger and better.

I once lived in a nice suburban neighborhood. I love porch sitting, and though there wasn't room for a traditional porch, we built a deck in the front of the house, outfitted with chairs to sit and enjoy the day. No other home on the street had any sort of porch or deck, just bare, empty lawns. I sat on the deck and watched cars come down our street. As one approached, one of several garage doors in the homes around us would rise automatically. The car would slip into the garage, the door would shut behind it, and that would be the last I saw of that car or neighbor until the garage opened again the next day and the car drove out for the morning's commute.

All of this—the dependence on cars, the bad city planning to make room for them, the quiet homes isolated in large, faceless neighborhoods—helped to create a loss of the sense of community. This is exacerbated by the worship of individualism in our society. America has long promoted the belief/myth that "anyone who works hard can pull themselves up by the bootstraps" and achieve success. There is truth to this, but over time it has fostered an economic model that only emphasizes "looking out for number one." This emphasis on the individual at the expense of the collective has caused many of us to insulate ourselves from each other. People in trouble from sickness, economic stress, and loneliness often suffer in isolation while those next-door remain oblivious.

Caught in the daily struggle to maintain what's ours, we forget what is also ours: our community, and our neighbors. Instead of a safe haven and place of well-being, in our isolation and debt our homes can feel like houses of detention. We have a great need to become a culture that values interdependence instead of worshiping independence. Because the fact is, though we pretend we are independent, we are all very much dependent on everyone else doing what they do to keep the lights on, the food growing and the businesses open.

A good home and a well-designed neighborhood should encourage, not discourage, interaction among neighbors. This is rare in today's suburban neighborhoods.

Despite all the emphasis over the last thirty years on expensive, larger homes, according to author David Wann three-fourths of Americans say they'd give up their dream homes to live in a great neighborhood. What makes a neighborhood great? This question, says Wann, is really asking, "What do we value the most?"

In an article in Urban Land Magazine, Fred Kent wrote, "The mixed-use developments that have predominated in the past few decades have focused primarily on shopping destinations—malls, strip centers, and lifestyle centers—and have failed to produce places that anchor and define communities. Cultural and educational institutions such as museums, libraries, and schools have frequently been developed in isolation, cut off from one another and from their downtowns, lacking public spaces and the surrounding uses that could make them gathering places and sustain them economically."

And finally, with perhaps a touch of hyperbole, from the book *The Geography of Nowhere* by James Howard Kunstler: "Thirty years ago Lewis Mumford said of post-World War II development, 'the end product is an encapsulated life, spent more and more in a motor car or within the cabin of darkness before a television set. The whole wicked, sprawling, megalopolitan mess,' he gloomily predicted, 'would completely demoralize mankind and lead to nuclear holocaust.'" There's some incentive for us. If we don't get to work creating better communities, we'll be nuked.

A good neighborhood should invoke a feeling of inclusiveness. Lots of homes are sold using the word "exclusive." In marketing we take that word to mean special, or above average, but it means just what it says; exclusive means others are excluded. A feeling of inclusiveness goes a long way to creating a happy environment and sense of belonging to something larger than individual houses. A feeling of attachment to a place is crucial.

A good neighborhood needs public spaces that encourage people mingling and sharing their lives and ideas. It's not so much about the dollars spent on the homes, it's about the richness of life and the feeling that we have an obligation to, and can receive the benefits of, a common interest in the well-being of our surroundings and our neighbors.

Creating car-free zones are something that is catching on in towns and cities across our nation and in Europe. These zones encourage people to walk or bike to do their errands whenever possible. Perhaps to make these changes it will mean that we will have to think things through a little more, maybe give up some convenience to create a better overall situation. In America we don't like to give things up. We're ingrained with a sense of entitlement and privilege, but it may be time to look beyond that, and when we do, we may be surprised to find we like the new way of doing things. As James Howard Kunstler wrote, "Rather than feel that something has been taken away from us, we would be wiser to see that something may be given back to us; a place to live and work in that we really love and care about and want to stay in, and don't feel compelled to flee from."

A long-term perspective would show a great benefit to making sure that everyone in our communities is working together to ensure that there is enough for everyone, creating a sort of community safety net. This includes shifting our support from mega-corporate entities to smaller, local businesses run by individuals in our own communities, getting to know our neighbors and actively participating by encouraging our local governments to create safe, people-friendly spaces throughout our cities. A long-term perspective reveals that working far from home, pumping dollars into giant corporate interests and isolating ourselves from each other ultimately creates a disconnect from community, the fullness of life and happiness. It's time to leave our houses, get out of our cars and get to know one another.

When there is a feeling of community and belonging, people have more incentive to do the right thing by themselves, each other and their environment. They want to live up to what's expected of them. It's easier to be a jerk in a faceless, unknown crowd. No one holds us accountable. Las Vegas, the town that is the poster child on so many levels of how not to do things, markets their city this way with their slogan "What happens in Vegas, stays in Vegas." What they're telling you is that if you go there no one will know you, so you can act out your worst instincts and be as depraved as you wish, without consequences. The same principle applies in our other large, faceless and anonymous cities. If no one knows you—if you're just another nameless individual with no connection to the whole—and you know or care about nobody else, why bother doing the right thing? No one else seems to be.

It's difficult to try to live a better life, or make even a small sacrifice to a larger group if it feels like you're the only one doing it. It seems pointless to pick up litter or conserve anything while standing in the middle of a society that seems to offer no reward for any of those things. As the fumes from another bus hit you, your little gesture of bringing your own reusable cup can seem idiotic and maybe even a little pathetic. The thought rises unbidden: there's nothing I can do to change this. My one little act is as futile as hurling a rock at an advancing panzer division, or the proverbial fart in a windstorm. But peer pressure, the thing we teach our children to resist, is very powerful when used for the common good. When enough people start acting with hope and compassion instead of talking about it and take action for the long-term good, we can make good change happen and transform our communities.

5

THE UNITED STATES OF GENERICA

I watched my country turn into a coast-to-coast strip mall, and I cried out in a song. If we could do all this in thirty years then please, please tell me ya'll, why does good change take so long?

Greg Brown, *The Poet Game*

NOT LONG AGO ONE OF THE JOYS OF TRAVELING across the United States was seeing and experiencing different places. When you crossed a state line, or sometimes even a county line, things changed, sometimes a lot. Towns looked different and restaurants served local food that was different from what you ate at home. Local customs were different than what you left behind. You could find a souvenir at the local store that personified that region and acted as a locally made memento of your visit. Stopping at local diners or trucks stops along the way, you could watch the menus change as you traveled. The closer you got to Kansas the more likely it was that you could order things like biscuits and gravy, which hadn't been on the menu at the last stop. If you took a southern route, you knew you were getting there when you stopped to eat and saw grits on the menu. It's not like you had a choice; you ate the local fare or you didn't eat. You could meet people with backgrounds and experiences vastly different from what you had known all your life, with different stories to tell and different perspectives of what it means to be an American.

This rich diversity of customs, foods, crafts and local quirks was what made it fun to visit new places. You could experience Texas barbeque hot off the grill, Chicago blues straight from the saxophone, New England lobster caught that day and Florida oranges right from the tree. Every state had its own offerings. But you usually had to actually go to these places to experience the real thing. Going to the store in a new place could be an adventure. When you shopped in these unknown stores you would encounter brands you hadn't seen before with unfamiliar labels. You felt like you were away from home.

Over the past thirty or forty years things have changed. Our nation, and to a certain extent our world, have experienced a sort of homogenization, a blurring of the idiosyncrasies and unique qualities that defined one state or one region from another until in many cases one place looks the same as pretty much any other place.

I live in Santa Rosa, in Northern California, and occasionally make a trip south down Highway 101which runs the length of California. Along the way I pass through many small towns, from Salinas to Gonzales, King City to Atascadero. Zipping along the road as I pass these towns, one thing stands out: every single town I pass through has the same strip mall alongside the freeway. They actually look like the exact same strip mall, all designed in the modern strip mall fashion, with the same combinations of pastel brick red, light yellow or sage green stucco exteriors, and the same endlessly-repeated corporate logos on the signs above the freeway. Home Depot, Walmart, Petco, Starbucks, Bed, Bath & Beyond, Target, Best Buy, Costco, Borders, Barnes & Noble, Lowes, Michael's. I could go on for a long time. Then there are the fast food outlets that accompany these stores: McDonald's, Burger King, Wendy's, In and Out Burger, Jack in the Box, Subway—you get the picture.

Driving along, when I would see another strip mall, I would start to think about pulling over to check a map to make sure I hadn't been driving in circles. How, I wondered, could I have been traveling all this time yet still keep passing the exact same strip mall? How many Starbucks will it take until we're satisfied? How many McDonald's? How many Walmarts? When will it end?

The truth is that in modern America, it won't end. It never ends. On a road trip across our great nation, when you get hungry and pull off the highway to eat—whether you're in Duluth, Phoenix, Kansas City, Tampa, Seattle, or New Orleans—you will find the same litany of fast food joints waiting there at virtually every freeway off ramp. The food you order will be exactly the same as in any other outlet, anywhere in the country. You have to really look if you want to experience local cuisine, because true local cuisine has almost become a thing of the past in America. Even sit-down restaurants have taken the corporate route with Appleby's, Red Lobster, Chili's, Outback Steakhouse, International House of Pancakes, Denny's, and so many others, each with the same laminated menu offering the same things in every store from Atlantic City to Sacramento. After you eat, if you're ready for a latte, no matter where you are there'll be a Starbucks nearby. They have 7,950 stores in the U.S. and over 11,200 worldwide. California alone has over 2000.

The Walmart around the corner is selling the exact same stuff you can buy at any Walmart anywhere in the country. If you're done travelling for the day, you can find an identical Best Western, Holiday Inn, Motel Six, or any one of many corporate motel/hotel chains. I once heard someone say that the Holiday Inn rooms are so alike in every state that he once checked into his room in Dallas and found his toenail clipping on the floor next to the nightstand just where he'd left it in San Diego.

While on your trip through modern America, if you buy a souvenir, like a snow globe in New York with a model of the statue of liberty in it, or perhaps a spoon rest in Kansas shaped and painted to look like a corn cob, you will probably find the words "Made in China" printed neatly somewhere on the back of your keepsake. Unique, regional souvenirs that are actually made in the area are nearly a thing of the past. (Actually, "Made in China" is not a new thing. In the 13th century, during the reign of the Mongol leader Kublai Khan, craftsmen in China were carving images of the Madonna and the Christ child out of ivory and shipping them west to be sold to Christians in Europe).

In just over one generation our country has become, in the words of my son Andrew, The United States of Generica. From coast to coast our towns have morphed into one big shopping complex, with the same stores everywhere you look. What we observed about the suburbs in the last chapter we can also see across the entire land; there is no "there" there. Today, every place in America offers the same foods, products, signage, expectations and experience across a wide spectrum of daily life.

With so much emphasis on shopping and consuming, we have allowed corporations to run rampant until they collectively would seem to define our national identity. If there's one thing a visitor to America will take away with them after a trip across our country, it's images of Walmart or McDonalds. A visitor could be excused for imagining that, despite all our talk about freedom and opportunity, in the end huge corporations and incessant shopping are essentially what we're all about. A huge share of our consumer spending has been captured by a shrinking number of mega corporations with one goal in mind—profit. These huge companies have managed to insinuate themselves into nearly every corner of our lives.

This inundation of mega corporations throughout our country has had some profound affects on communities across the nation. Unknown shareholders and corporate managers over the last several decades have become the arbiters of the economic well-being of communities they have never visited and know little about except the profitability of the local demographic. In her book, *Big Box Swindle*, author Stacy Mitchell likens this to a "modern variation on the old European colonial system, which was designed not to build economically viable and self-reliant communities, but to extract their wealth and resources."

Though the chain-store phenomenon is highly visible today, it's not a new thing in America. One of the earliest chain stores, the Great Atlantic and Pacific Tea Company, better known as the A & P, was started in 1859 with one small store in Manhattan. The chain grew to hundreds of outlets by the early 1900s. The A & P was the Walmart of its day, though even at its peak it only captured one quarter as much of American consumer dollars as Walmart has captured today.

As the business model of chain stores grew popular, many other familiar names appeared on the landscape. Woolworths, Sears and Roebuck, JC Penney, Piggly Wiggly, Kroger Grocery Store, and many others became well known across the country. In the words of Ellen Ruppel Shell in her book *Cheap: The*

High Cost of Discount Culture, "These stores were free agents without loyalty to any particular community, and they held no loyalty to any particular supplier. Price was the determining factor in most of their transactions."

Like today, there were consumer groups protesting the infiltration of their communities by these large corporations. Citizen's groups in the early 1900s rallied against chain stores unfairly driving down wages and hurting local businessmen. They were also concerned about too much economic power being concentrated into the hands of so few. Sound familiar? John Hargreaves, an early president of the Retail Merchant's Association, complained that cut-rate prices "reduced the value of labour, and have destroyed the purchasing power of many classes, thereby affecting all classes." Shopkeepers in the early 1900s who advertised low prices to attract business were scorned by many as gutter merchants. Chain stores in particular came under fire as citizens coast to coast banded together to halt what they considered a vicious and cutthroat corporate invasion, but the chains kept on coming, growing by 300 percent in the 1920s alone. A handful of local governments attempted to thwart their growth by levying high taxes and fees, limiting the number of outlets a chain could open in a particular area, and in some cases, even trying to outlaw chain stores entirely.

Like today, the companies countered with the claim that their success proved that they were offering their customers the one thing that counted above all others, lower prices. Their power over us seemed intractable. Since the early 1900s, however, concerned citizen's groups and local governments have stopped the construction and encroachment of hundreds of big-box developments, proving that while the mega-retailer's pockets are deep and their influence great, they are not unstoppable.

Though it appears that big-box discount chains are the inevitable result of wise, price-conscious consumer spending and bring economic growth and prosperity, in reality they often cost the communities in which they do business much more than any jobs or money they bring. As many are realizing, lower prices on the shelves often means higher prices on other important things, such as the loss of a stable local economy, the inability to earn a living wage, and ultimately the unraveling of the very fabric of our communities.

When people shop at chain stores, their dollars, which used to circulate locally to fuel the local economy, leave the area, enriching owners and shareholders far away. Consider this: for every dollar spent at a corporate chain store, 15 cents stays to circulate in the local economy. For every dollar spent in a locally owned business, 45 cents stays in the community, a difference of 150 percent.

Walmart has grown exponentially since 1990, taking about ten percent of every dollar spent on just about everything in the United States. The top 10 mega retailers now command about 30 percent of all consumer spending, while hundreds of thousands of smaller, locally-owned, family businesses have disappeared, the very small family businesses that created the American small-town dream in the first place. Ellen Ruppel Shell states, "Discount chains not only put untold numbers of small retailers out of business, they reshaped the American demographic. Since retail traditionally had one of the lowest median rates of pay, the expansion of discount retailers that paid even lower wages contributed to a spurt in poorly paid jobs."

We like the convenience and the low prices, but almost anyone you ask will tell you that they hate the blight of corporate logos looming over every landscape and the inundation of fast-food joints on virtually every corner. Nobody seems to actually like huge, impersonal strip malls. Nobody likes dealing with the traffic to get there, yet we continue to patronize these businesses even though we have a choice to shop elsewhere. If we took the time to give the matter some serious thought using our best long-term thinking skills, most of us would choose to shop elsewhere in order to bolster and support our local economy. Despite the perceived right-now savings garnered at these stores, there are many hidden costs to shopping at big-box stores or chain stores that, over the long run, end up costing us—and our communities—much more than what we save at the cash register.

The takeover of our towns' economies by large, faceless, corporate interests robs us of community, weakens the local economy and makes us vulnerable to decisions made from afar, with little or no regard to the consequences of those decisions on our corner of the world. There are compelling long-term reasons for rethinking our current paradigm of corporate gigantism. Much of the power to shape, control or even end corporate influence lies with us collectively as consumers.

It's not always easy making the choice to forgo shopping at chain discount stores in favor of supporting local businesses. Marketing is powerful and giant corporations are very good at it. Each day, everywhere we go, we are bombarded with messages from dozens of corporate mega stores, each trying to catch our attention and divert our dollars their way. We may like to believe that we can ignore them or that we are immune to their efforts, but if we live in America we can't help but absorb these messages unless we're in a coma (and sometimes it seems that all those ads are enough to put you in that coma!) Being used to absorbing lots of marketing messages is not the same as not being able to resist them. You have to pay attention and think carefully when you spend your money, because—and you'll hear me say this more than once—every dollar you spend is a vote for the kind of life you want for yourself and your society.

It's sometimes difficult to comprehend how hard corporations work and how much they spend to get your attention. In 2004, according to their annual report, Walmart spent $1.4 billion dollars on advertising alone. That's one thousand four hundred million dollars spent just to entice us in or keep us coming back, mostly by offering lower prices. The larger a corporation gets, the larger the bulk buys it can make from its suppliers; the larger the purchase, the lower the cost per item to the store, and presumably to the customer. At its simplest, this is why a company like Walmart can out-compete local businesses that are not on the same tier when it comes to buying power and too often manages to drive them out of business.

People may complain when a Walmart or other big-box store comes to town, but when the new Walmart opens its doors the people will come, in spite of feeling vaguely uneasy about forgoing their tried and true local businesses. Most of us who shop at Walmart or other large chain discount stores do so because we think we'll save a couple of bucks on a toaster or a few cents on any number of other items, because that's what the game is all about, saving a few bucks, right?

Before we beat ourselves up for chasing small discounts that allow mega corporations to take over our communities, it's worth taking a look at the fact that the huge rise in the power of big-box retailers was made possible in the first place by favorable zoning laws and huge tax breaks provided by local governments, lured by the promises of these large retailers to bring jobs to town. Where some municipalities attempted to pass laws and levy heavy taxes to stop the spread of giant discount retailers in their communities, in most cases local governments courted them shamelessly, imagining that these businesses would bring prosperity and a strong tax base.

In the 1950s, new tax laws in thousands of communities were put in place to provide incentives to large retailers to bring their businesses to these towns, using tax dollars as a form of corporate welfare. These tax incentives provided and continue to provide billions of dollars in subsidized tax savings to these mega retailers. They are sometimes referred to as the "Geoffrey Loophole," named after the Toys R Us mascot.

After providing these tax breaks, along with other incentives including lax environmental and infrastructure standards on construction of their huge "boxes," many small communities found that instead of a windfall from sales taxes and a boon in employment, they experienced smaller, core businesses in the community closing their doors forever, unable to compete with the aggressive, predatory pricing put forth by the leviathan they invited into their midst. These super-large retailers force out their smaller competitors by being bigger, not better. The jobs they offer are low paying and do not provide medical benefits, and communities often find their hospital emergency rooms overrun by citizens who cannot afford health care and end up using the ER as their primary care facility.

Mega-retailers are skillful at keeping employees working just under the number of hours that would require them to provide medical or retirement benefits, forcing many of these working poor to sign up for food stamps or Medicare. They squelch any attempt by their employees to form unions. When employees at a Canadian Walmart successfully formed the first-ever Walmart workers' union the company shut the store down, putting hundreds of people out of work.

After jumping through hoops to entice mega-retailers these towns find, in the words of Stacey Mitchell, "…they are the de facto serfs of the lord retailer, utterly vulnerable to the company's decisions regarding local laws, wages and employment; always having to jump through hoops under the threat that the large company may pick up and move to the next town."

The problem of corporate encroachment is not confined to mega-retailers with giant stores. Corporate entities with smaller footprints such as Starbucks coffee also take their toll. I used to publish a local magazine in the Napa Valley wine country of Northern California geared toward the residents of the Napa Valley, covering local events and happenings, people and business. At that time Starbucks was running a series of television ads touting their stores as the "local meeting place," or "your community gathering place," in an attempt to head off any resentment of their over-the-top presence in nearly every community. Despite their ads claiming that Starbucks was all about being "local," when I approached the managers about distributing my local magazine in their stores, I was told by all of them that publications distributed in their stores must first be approved by their corporate headquarters, which was over a thousand miles away. Despite claiming to be a part of my community they would not allow my magazine, which really was part of the community, to be made available to their customers.

I share this story because it illustrates the fact that although corporate stores claim to be part of and care about the communities where they do business, their interest for the most part doesn't extend much past the profitability of each store. Their corporate guidelines are put in place by absentee owners thousands of miles away who know little or nothing about the communities they "serve." Raise your hand if you know of a local coffee shop that was put out of business or taken over by a Starbucks.

Corporations are aware that there is resentment and blowback from communities, so they make concerted efforts to change their image from faceless corporate imperialism to that of a benign, caring neighbor. Starbucks is not the only one to claim that their company is a community gathering place. This hijacking of the "Main Street" image is common. When a new, sprawling retail complex is built on the edge of another town, they are often given names like, "The Commons," or "Village," just as sprawling ticky-tack suburban developments are given names like, "Pine Meadows," though there is not a pine or a meadow to be found anywhere. These attempts at creating a false sense of community extend to fashioning strip malls in the style of old-fashioned Main Street scenes, replete with faux gas lights, quaint signage, and false fronts like a Hollywood movie set. Underneath the façade lurk the same corporate entities found everywhere else. Starbucks even changed the names of some of their stores to monikers like 15th Avenue Coffee and Tea, going as far as removing the well-known Starbucks logo in an attempt to better blend into the local landscape.

In the last chapter we looked at suburban sprawl, that soulless spread of tract homes and strip malls that defines so much of America. Big retail developments exacerbate this sprawl wherever they appear and it has been shown that the larger a store or development is, the farther people will travel to shop there. Consumers will happily drive long distances, burning gas and choking the roads, to shop at a giant retail store. Huge retailers spend millions to understand consumers' motivations and desires (they probably know us better than we do) and capitalize on this, competing with one another to build the largest, most conspicuous stores possible.

This has, says Stacy Mitchell, set off a kind of development arms race—a never-ending quest to outsize the competitors and undercut Main Street. Our culture and quest of discounts has created the perfect conditions for big-box retailers to compete with each other by building larger and larger stores to lure people away from their city centers. The discounts they offer often turn out to be negligible and not worth the added costs of time and gasoline to get there.

The number of viable, locally owned neighborhood businesses in our communities affect how much we drive and how much we use public transportation. Susan Handy, who studies travel behavior at the University of California, Davis, found that how often people walked to do their errands was tied to how close the stores were and how many choices there were. People in neighborhoods that had a healthy number of small, local stores drove 42 percent less to shop than similar neighborhoods that did not have a thriving, populated downtown. But our habits of driving long distances to go shopping in chain stores are hard to break.

The amount of retail space per person in the U.S. doubled in the 15 years between 1990 and 2005. To accommodate the cars bringing the frenzied shoppers to these retail paradises, for every square foot of retail space another three to four feet was paved for parking. Studies show that when a new Walmart came to a town, rather than bring more business and invigorating the economy, 84 percent of the sales were simply shifting dollars away from local merchants. The good news is that recent signs have begun to show some positive shifts in the mega-retailer dominance of our nation. Traditional "mom and pop" stores are beginning to thrive again in many parts of the country as more people reject the big-box mentality. Locally owned retail now makes up more than 70 percent of all businesses in America.

Local merchants are part of the community and have a vested interest in the welfare of their towns and customers. If they alienate their customers, they can't shut the store and move on to the next place; their stores are part and parcel of their home, their lives and their livelihood. Local merchants are much more likely to do business with the local bank, local craftsmen, local suppliers and shop locally themselves. They consistently advertise in local publications. For local merchants, relationships and trust are as much a part of doing business as is profit. They are a strong thread in the fabric of their communities.

I recently bought a book at an independent bookstore in my home town, a much-loved, somewhat unorganized, messy small-town bookstore where you can browse for hours, where the owner and employees know and love books as much as their customers. Their inventory is not computerized. If you are looking for an obscure title they'll point you in the right general direction. After that it's up to you. This of course leads to long hours of exploring of dusty shelves and quite often, serendipitous surprises. Anyway, after getting my book home I realized it was the wrong version of the book I wanted. Later, in the bookstore again without the book I had purchased, I mentioned to them that I had bought the wrong book. The owner pulled the book I wanted off the shelf, handed it to me and asked me to bring the other one by the next time I was in. Nothing was signed; no money changed hands. He let me walk out with the new book. Of course, I made a point of quickly returning the other book to him as soon as I could, as he knew I would.

You could never do that at a discount chain bookstore. With absentee owners, no one has any authority to make decisions like that. Employees have their manual and are trained to push the right pre-programmed buttons on the cash register. There is no room for the human element, and in the long run the human element is what it's all about.

People thrive on relationships and love to do business with people they know and trust. There is nothing more in line with the story of America than owning your own business. There was a time when a man or woman could buy a house and raise a family on the wages earned as an employee at a small, local business. Knowing your local baker or shopkeeper is part of the richness of belonging to a local community. Not only do you know them, they know you, your habits, your likes and dislikes. They ask about your kids. In this type of relationship the balance of power is fair and equal. You need your merchant, and he or she needs you. The shopkeeper has little incentive to increase profits by gouging his customers and the customer has little incentive to take the merchant's profit by demanding lower and lower prices. It's symbiotic. If a local shopkeeper ran his business with only profit in mind at the expense of his customers' experience and satisfaction, he would not be in business for long.

Despite this correlation between where we spend our dollars and the health of our communities, we are conditioned to seek discounts. Many of us still flock to distant mega-discounters even when we know it's hurting our own local businesses.

It's time to take the long-term view, and translate our understanding of the harm mega-retailers inflict on our communities into action. Many parts of the country now have organizations that promote shopping locally. Go on the Internet and type "shop local" along with the name of your town or county and see what you get.

How can you alone making the decision to shop locally have any affect on the encroachment of mega-retailers? Watching throngs of people going into the local Walmart, it may seem like your choice to shop locally and perhaps spend a little more won't change anything. As in so many other aspects of our lives, one person may have little power, but collectively we can have a huge affect on any number of things, including revitalizing our local communities. Like a huge oil tanker at top speed, heavy with momentum, mega-retailers have charted a course straight through the center of our local economies, and, like an oil tanker, it can be difficult to slow or turn. Individually we cannot do much, but together we can lay the awesome weight of our collective economic power on the rudder of this corporate behemoth, and gradually change the course of their business and the economic well-being of our communities and our lives. It's our choice, but we must do it together.

Bear with me if you will while I tell you a short story from a cartoon I once saw. I don't usually cite cartoon episodes to back up my arguments, but I take my wisdom where I find it. This cartoon episode was from the popular animated television show, South Park, a show rife with social commentary, albeit delivered in an often acerbic, socially unacceptable manner.

In this particular episode, titled "Something Walmart This Way Comes," Walmart opened a mega-store in the small town of South Park. As in so many towns where Walmart makes an appearance, the citizenry rose up in indignation, and groups organized to force the store to close. But when these concerned citizens went into the Walmart to voice their complaints they found themselves captivated by price tags offering amazing deals on all sorts of things. "Screwdrivers for a dollar ninety-nine!" they exclaimed, then found themselves in the checkout line with a pile of stuff they hadn't intended to buy, because no matter how much they hated what Walmart represented they couldn't resist the low prices.

The children of the community, originally proud of their parents' stand against the mega-retailer, were horrified to find their mothers and fathers succumbing to the low prices. They decided to take on Walmart themselves, to save their parents and their town. By this point in the cartoon the big-box store was being depicted as a malevolent, sentient predator, the building itself breathing and laughing as it captured the retail souls of the towns' residents and destroyed the local economy. In order to destroy the beast the children had to find "the heart of Walmart" and drive a sword into it.

Fighting their way into the store, stepping around adults who were shopping like zombies, the children came across an old man and told him they were there to slay Walmart by driving a sword into its heart. The old man smiled, stepped aside and pointed to a television. There, he told them, behind that plasma screen TV is the heart of Walmart. The children prepared their swords to kill the beast and they flung the TV aside.

Instead of the beating heart of the beast, they found a mirror and stood there staring at their own reflections. The old man smiled. "You are the heart of Walmart," he told them, explaining that Walmart couldn't be successful without "you," the consumer.

The inconvenient truth is that if we don't like Walmart or any other discount retailers encroaching on our communities, we are the ones that must do something about it. It's up to us, individually and collectively. If we see ourselves as victims we will feel powerless as our communities are stolen from us. As soon as we decide to take our collective power back we will be unstoppable. It cannot happen without our consent and our participation.

Long-term thinking and shopping locally go hand in hand. Shopping locally keeps dollars in our neighborhoods. Local businesses help create and sustain the character of our towns and communities—those quirks and special features that make them unique, not just knock-offs of every town around ours.

You'll usually get better service from local businesses because they understand their customers' needs and wants, and have a stake in keeping good relationships with the public.

Small, local businesses are collectively the largest employer in the nation, and account for the lion's share of job growth. Local businesses are far less likely to pull up stakes and take their business and jobs elsewhere. Small businesses create more choice of products than homogenized chain stores. Shopping locally helps the environment and helps keep down congestion, habitat loss, pollution, and sprawl.

Local businesses tend to support local non-profits who report an average of 350 percent more support from local businesses than they do from non-local businesses. Local businesses need less infrastructure, have less need for large outlays of public services and are run by people who have a stake in the towns in which they do business. They make decisions with that in mind.

It's up to us. We cannot wait for corporations to do the right thing. They won't. They are under a legal mandate to do whatever it takes to increase profits for their shareholders, no matter the cost to communities, the planet or individual lives. If the CEOs of these corporations do not do everything in their power to increase profits, they can be sued by shareholders and removed from their position.

No matter how large the problem or how insignificant our efforts may seem in the short run, over the long run, if we stick together we can shift the dominant economic paradigm of greed, power and profit, to one of balance, fairness and a mindset of making decisions for the common good, and for the long-term best interest of all.

Our culturally induced penchant for rampant consumerism is a large part of what drives us to continue patronizing these big-box stores. Which brings us to the subject of our next chapter.

6

THE BEST THINGS IN LIFE AREN'T THINGS

You can never get enough of what you don't need to make you happy.

Eric Hoffer

Be as simple as you can be; you will be astonished to see how uncomplicated and happy your life can become.

Paramahansa Yogananda

The only reason a great many American families don't own an elephant is that they have never been offered an elephant for a dollar down and easy weekly payments.

Mad Magazine

The story goes something like this: In 1949, a businessman named Frank McNamara who was head of Hamilton Credit Corporation, went to dinner in New York with Alfred Bloomingdale, McNamara's long-time friend and grandson of the founder of Bloomingdale's Department store. When they were presented with the bill, McNamara realized that he had forgotten his wallet and had no cash to pay. Embarrassed, he had to call his wife to bring him money. The experience left an impression on him. There should be a viable alternative to cash, he thought, because he couldn't have been the only one to find himself in the position of having money in the bank, but none in his pocket.

He and some partners talked it over and came up with an idea that they felt would catch on—a credit card that could be used at multiple locations. Originally it was marketed toward travelling salesmen who were required to dine out often to entertain clients; thus, they christened it the Diners' Club Card. The idea was that restaurants would submit the bills to Diners' Club, who would pay them and bill their members. Diners' Club charged a percentage of the sale to the businesses that accepted the cards as payment, and a small yearly membership fee to the members.

When I first encountered that story my initial thought was, well, if Mr. McNamara had forgotten his wallet, then even if he had a credit card he would have had the same problem, because it would presumably have been at home in his wallet and he would have had to call his wife anyway. But let's not let that get in the way of a good tale. At any rate, their idea caught on rapidly, and in a couple of years Diners' Club had over 20,000 members, making the Diners' Club card the first credit card in use on a wide scale.

Other companies had issued versions of credit cards before this, but those cards locked customers into doing business only with the company that issued the card, such as department store cards or gas station cards. Some businesses resisted accepting Diners' Club at first, fearing it would compete with their own credit cards, but over time most got on board.

The first credit cards, including Diners' Club, are more accurately described as charge cards rather than credit cards, since the balance had to be paid off each month. Customers were not allowed to spend beyond their ability to pay the charges off at regular intervals until Diners' Club and other cards such as BankAmericard, which later became VISA, conceived and put into place that alluring and dangerous concept known as revolving credit. Cardholders could pay their balance in full at the end of each month or make a minimum payment and let the balance ride. Which do you think most customers chose to do each month?

This of course carried the risk of customers getting over their head in debt. The balance that was not paid off each month was carried over and added to the principal of the loan, offering more freedom and flexibility to all the players. It also opened that Pandora's box that has come to define life in America and the western world. For the first time in history a large portion of the population could easily spend more than they made at any given time. No money? No problem. Put it on your credit card and pay it off over time.

Until this point in history, when people wanted or needed something, they had to either save up until they could afford it or go without. Not that credit was a new thing. It had existed for thousands of years, but not for individual consumers making small purchases. Mortgages, business loans and these types of credit were common. But with the advent of credit cards, meals, entertainment, new washing machines, televisions, furniture, clothes and kitchen appliances all sang their sweet siren song of easy credit terms, a song difficult to resist when we were incessantly bombarded with advertising telling us not to resist. It's all good, the credit card companies told us. You can buy anything you want with an easy, affordable minimum monthly payment; there's no need to wait, you can fulfill your desires right now. We were suddenly all like kids in a candy store; we could have as much as we wanted. As it turns out, we wanted a lot.

Man 1: My wife had her credit card stolen three months ago.

Man 2: Did you call the police?

Man 1: No, the thief is spending less than my wife did.

At some point it may have been wise for credit card holders to ask themselves: wait a minute, this is great in the short term, but if I keep making purchases with this card and only make the minimum payment each month, what will happen in the long term? Hmmmm...The answer of course was and is obvious: increasing and ultimately crippling debt. Few asked that question though. Humans are not inclined to think long term. Instead, as they purchased more and more with their credit cards and made only minimum payments, those minimum payments climbed as the prior month's balance and interest were added to the current month's obligation, increasing the debt and the minimum payment. A financial snowball in reverse. Instead of their wealth growing, their debt grew. Each time they made a minimum payment instead of paying down the principal, it was like taking a shovel and digging their hole a little deeper.

Many spent on credit until they could barely afford the minimum payments, forcing them to stop. The evil truth was that even if they didn't buy one more thing and only made their minimum payment, their debt would continue growing. They were trapped. Since they could barely afford the minimum payment, they couldn't pay more to bring down the balance. The interest combined with the previous balance carried over continued to increase their debt and their real-life nightmare in an endlessly repeating pattern of deeper debt. Soon, many were in so deep they could no longer see any financial light. Making those minimum payments felt like paying the "vig" to a loan shark. Sound familiar? Are you one of the trapped?

Statistically, it's likely that you are. According to a survey done by the Federal Reserve Bank of Boston in 2010, there are 609.8 million credit cards held by U.S. consumers, and the average credit card holder has 3.5 cards to his or her name as of the end of 2008. Of those households with credit card debt, the average debt was $15,788, being charged an average interest rate of 14.35 percent. According to the same survey, total consumer debt in the U.S. is $2.4 trillion. Of that, the total revolving debt, 98 percent of which is on credit cards, is $852.6

billion. According to the U.S. Census Bureau, by 2010 181 million Americans were projected to have a credit card.

According to myfico.com, "on average, today's consumer has a total of 13 credit obligations on record at a credit bureau. These include credit cards (such as department store charge cards, gas cards, and bank cards) and installment loans (auto loans, mortgage loans, student loans, etc.). Of these 13 credit obligations, nine are likely to be credit cards and four are likely to be installment loans."

Credit cards have become as ubiquitous as the air we breathe. They confer status, as any American Express Gold Card commercial will tell you. They bring "rewards" such as airline miles or bonus points that can be redeemed for even more fabulous merchandise. Credit cards keep us buying things whether we need them or not, and that in turn keeps the economy chugging along. On the dark side, for far too many people they are the last resort, a life ring used in desperation to pay for essentials like groceries, rent, taxes or hospital bills, and to put off the inevitable reckoning until some later date. Buying on credit drives businesses and keeps people employed, but keeping factories open and the economy going by consumers accruing debt is not sustainable in the long term.

The question is not why do we use credit cards. The question is why do so many Americans feel the need to over consume until they are choked in debt, struggling to manage and maintain their possessions? Especially in light of the fact that it's completely avoidable. Those numbingly similar strip malls in every town in America couldn't exist if we didn't keep going back and buying everything they sell whether or not we need it. It's worth stopping to ask, what are we trying to accomplish by working so hard to acquire so much? Americans work harder than any other people in the world. Why do we seem to only consider others or ourselves a success if they or we have lots of stuff?

It's very simple: in America, we are taught from a young age that good citizenship equals rampant consumerism. Here in the Land of the Free, we have one general yardstick to measure success: money. When we say a person is successful it doesn't mean that he or she is happy, nice, worthy, honest, content, friendly, generous or a good person. When we say someone is successful, we mean that he or she has money. (Even if you don't actually have money, you can still surround yourself with the trappings of money through the magic of—insert sound of heavenly choir here—credit.)

You almost never see images of millionaires without their limos, yachts or private jets. Late night infomercials selling get-rich-quick schemes to sleepy television viewers always show the guy who is selling the scheme posing with fancy cars, giant homes overlooking the ocean, hot tubs full of bikini-clad women and the like. All with the promise that if you buy his get-rich program, you, too, can have all this—this stuff. The subtext to this messaging is this simple equation that we in America learn as young children and carry throughout our lives: money = stuff = happiness.

Does it?

In his book, *Deep Economy*, Bill McKibben points out that in western culture the idea of more and the idea of better exist side by side in most peoples' consciousness. He compared them to two birds, one called "More," and one called "Better," sitting next to each other on a branch in a tree. For a long time in our history if you threw one stone you could hit them both; More and Better came as one package. Anyone growing up in America is told repeatedly over a lifetime that more is, in fact, better. McKibben observes that for most of us in America, those two birds, More and Better, have moved farther apart in the tree. Now when we throw the rock and hit More, we only get More, and rarely find that things get Better. Many of us live our whole life with some pie-in-the-sky vision of how things will be the future when we finally have all the stuff we've always wanted and will finally be happy, in the process perhaps missing out on how good life is right now.

Of course, when the first American immigrants struggled to secure a foothold on the east coast and were dying in droves from lack of food and shelter, more would certainly have been better. If you're an eleven-year-old child in Sudan or Haiti and you have no food, clean water or shelter, more will always be better. Much of the world's population lives in abject poverty, with food insecurity a permanent part of their lives. Billions of fellow humans suffer daily from poor sanitation, exposure and malnutrition. For any of these people, more of anything—except perhaps more drought, war and food shortages—will make their lives better.

Our problem here is that we've taken the more-is-better theme to such extremes that acquiring more no longer brings us greater satisfaction; in fact it often brings the opposite. With worry, guilt, fear, debt, maintenance, storage and insurance coming on the heels of our purchases, complicating our lives and sapping our income, it lowers our feeling of well-being. Robert F. Kennedy said, in a 1968 speech, "...we seemed to have surrendered personal excellence and community values in the mere accumulation of material things."

Most of us are aware that if we don't continue to buy things our economy, national security and position in the world will swiftly decline. We have collectively trapped ourselves in this model of endlessly buying the latest product.

The truth is that many of us continue to believe that more is better, that buying the latest and greatest gadgets, clothes, cars, or whatever, will make us happier. We've been... well, brainwashed is perhaps too strong a word; but on second thought, perhaps not. We've been trained since early childhood to believe that acquiring more stuff will make us happier, but for most this has not turned out to be true. A famous story tells of a psychologist who was asked if he'd rather treat a rich man or a poor man. A rich man, he answered, because a rich man already knows that money won't buy him happiness.

I recently saw a commercial for a bank encouraging parents to get a new "credit card" for their young children. You load it with whatever amount you choose, the ad said, and it teaches your children about financial responsibility. As I watched I thought, no, that's a lie. It doesn't teach financial responsibility at all. A kid handed a card like that would have no connection to how the money got into the account, except that mom or dad put it there. They'd have no sense of working for it, or what it's worth. What a card like this will actually do is brainwash kids at an early age to believe that when you want to buy something, you pull out a card. Then, when they're eighteen they'll know how the system works and will be ready to start building their own life of debt.

Our financial system encourages us to be in debt. Despite what they say, our own government and the corporations that own and control it encourage accumulation not of wealth, but of debt. When we continue using credit to make purchases it drives our economy, keeps the profits rolling in and allows politicians to say how well we're all doing. Being in debt keeps us working to service that debt, or risk everything. When people are in debt they are afraid of losing their possessions, their security and their way of life. A person deep in debt is easy to control. They don't dare rock the boat for fear of having all their stuff taken away. The powers-that-be continue to tell us through incessant marketing that we can, even if we have no real wealth, share in the trappings of prosperity by using credit and building debt.

Parker Brothers recently came out with a version of the popular board game Monopoly that uses an electronic credit card machine instead of the old traditional paper Monopoly money for banking, again training children from a young age to think of credit as money—to pull out a card.

Many American kids get credit card offers in the mail as soon as they turn eighteen. Some contain large checks—ahem, loans. All you have to do is sign here and endorse the check, the letter says, and the money is yours. This practice is predatory and insidious. Imagine an eighteen-year-old girl in her dorm room far from home, with a check for 3 or 5 thousand dollars in her hand that magically appeared in the mail. No parents around, and for the first time she doesn't have to ask anyone for permission. Just sign and cash the check and she'll have thousands of dollars right now. How easy is that?

The fine print that the girl never reads explains that if she signs it she'll pay an astounding amount of interest, and that it will take her years to put a small dent in the amount owed. They will essentially own her for the rest of her life. If she ever manages to pay it off she will have paid many, many times the original amount borrowed.

There is no way her first purchases will be the only things she buys on easy credit terms over the next several years. She's going to need a car, clothes, a new smart phone. What about student loans? Welcome to adulthood in America, where long-term thinking is frowned upon. If we're doing it "right" we will start at a young age gathering as many possessions as possible, along with the lifelong debt and hassle that accompanies them. This financial foisting of today's problems onto the future is a microcosm of humanity's overall way of dealing with long-term issues. We don't.

One of the ironies of our obsession with consumerism is this: If you ask people what they think are the most important things in life, most will not say, "more stuff," or "more debt." What you will hear are likely to be simple, short answers such as family, love, peace, friendship, spirituality and health. We all know that money won't buy us happiness; this is simple, age-old grandmotherly wisdom. So what gives? Why do we continue to pursue that which not only doesn't bring happiness but often brings unhappiness?

Psychologist Richard Ryan points out that, "desire to have more and more material goods drives us into an ever more frantic pace of life. Not only must we work harder, but once possessing the goods we have to maintain, upgrade, replace, insure, and constantly manage them. Thus, materialists end up carrying an ever-heavier load that expands the energy necessary for living, loving, and learning."

When people reach that point where the foundational reality of their economic life is maintaining their debt, as so many millions of Americans have, they begin to understand that none of their purchases have made—or will make—them happier.

For many, that's when the American dream turns into the American nightmare, like a beautiful maiden who morphs into a hideous, cackling old crone before their eyes. By then it's often too late; they're trapped. That's when, as Boston Globe columnist Ellen Goodman put it, "Normal is getting dressed in clothes that you buy for work, driving through traffic in a car that you are still paying for, in order to get to the job that you need so you can pay for the clothes, car, and the house that you leave empty all day in order to afford to live in it."

I call this "feeding the monster," and for many it has become the main focus of life. Though our collective mind set tells us more is always better, I think we can agree that a person living in an $800,000 home is not necessarily twice as happy as a person who lives in a $400,000 home, and a person driving a Lexus isn't more fulfilled than a person driving a Chevy. In fact, the only thing we can surmise with certainty from the above examples is that the former in each case likely has a bigger payment.

We have allowed ourselves to be led into a world of consumerism where everything we have been told will make us happy has made us unhappy. We have been persuaded to go into debt to get things we don't need with money we don't have to attain satisfaction we never feel.

Sometimes we use one credit card to pay the balance on the next. We worry about our credit scores, kept by large, faceless corporations who have created a business out of thin air, a business of judging you, the consumer, by assigning you a number based on your past purchases and payment record. We are constantly sent messages to "fear" a low credit score. If your credit score is low, you are judged inadequate and not up to the task of buying more stuff.

There are myriad Web sites that let you check your credit score or take steps to improve it. I'm often struck by the irony that working yourself to death to maintain your credit score qualifies you for one thing: the right to go deeper into debt and work yourself to death paying that debt so your credit score won't be affected and you can qualify for more debt. It's all a bit crazy, isn't it? It's a well-laid trap. I realize I'm over-simplifying this, but...come on.

Have you ever noticed around the holidays that each night on the news the lead story is about how retail sales are going? Millions of us run out to the malls like rats on a treadmill, rack up more debt, then run home breathlessly and turn on the news to find out if we've been spending enough.

Many of us buy so much stuff that we can't fit it into our homes, so we need to store it elsewhere. Over the past 30 years the self-storage industry has been one of the fastest growing industries in the nation. On the edge of our suburbs we have the large, big-box strip malls, and just beyond those we have acres and acres of self-storage.

According to the Self-Storage Association, just over one in 10 American households rent storage space. It took 25 years to build their first billion square feet of storage space, and eight years to build their second billion. They are proud to point out that "There is a self-storage space inventory of approximately 19.5 square feet per U.S. household, and approximately 7.2 square feet of self storage space for every man, woman, and child in the nation, making it physically possible that every American could stand—all at the same time—under the total canopy of self-storage roofing."

What are we storing in these billions of square feet of storage space? Most of the things people store come down to old couches, that painting your wife made you take down, old boxes of plastic toys, parts from cars, old vacuum cleaners, piles of old National Geographic magazines, that set of chairs from the old table that had to be thrown away, etc.

There is a huge self-storage auction industry across this nation. When storage renters default on their payments, they cut the lock and let bidders look inside the space to see the goods. The highest bidder gets everything inside. Sometimes they find valuables, like an expensive vintage collection of baseball cards or a box of old coins. Mostly they get old couches and boxes of other peoples' junk. There is now a popular television show called "Storage Wars" which chronicles these hopeful bidders.

I know someone who put some things in storage "just for a while." About 15 years later she finally went in to do something with it and realized that it was all pretty much worthless. She had been paying about $140 a month for 15 years. For those without a calculator handy, that comes to just over $25,000.

This begs the question of why someone would continue shopping and buying things on credit when they already pay hundreds of dollars a month to store things they bought before but don't have enough room for, or enough interest in, to keep in their house. What will they do with the new stuff they buy? Rent another storage space?

Images of wealth and the wealthy are paraded in front of us constantly. Most of us struggle to get by, yet we turn people into celebrities for no other reason except they have a lot of money. We wag our finger at big business and its myopic vision that has profit as its only goal, but our popular culture doesn't reflect this. We worship wealth in our society. We turn fleshy, greedy narcissists like Donald Trump into celebrities simply because they are rich, famous for their skill at grabbing and keeping. We give vacuous celebrities like Paris Hilton their own TV shows because they are rich. We can't seem to get enough. Middle- and lower-income people come home from long days at work and plop down in front the TV to watch shows like "Lifestyles of the Rich and Famous," or "Who Wants to be a Millionaire?" We gaze glassy-eyed into this world of riches that we have been told is the ultimate goal of life. We grew up with the images of Little Orphan Annie and her benefactor, Daddy Warbucks, or Julia Roberts, who went from a street hooker to a woman of means when sugar daddy Richard Gere rescued her in the movie *Pretty Woman.*

Even our language reflects this. We say that so-and-so is "worth" so many millions of dollars. I believe language has power over the way we perceive the world. Is Donald Trump really "worth" more than your grandmother? Is Britney Spears really "worth" more than the volunteer at the food bank who helps others after his workday is through?

I am not saying that there is a cabal of evil people in a smoky room somewhere, plotting nefarious schemes to keep us dumbed down (though I'm not saying there's not), but I am saying the financial system has taken on a persona of its own and in order to continue it needs passive consumers to live fearfully and make buying decisions based on bad data and false promises.

Because we so often fail to think long term and believe that the trappings of materialism are the way to gauge our happiness, we have become a nation that can be controlled, as they used to say in ancient Rome, with "bread and circuses." Give us enough cheap food and entertainment and we will let you get away with just about anything. Our children are being fed a mental diet of fatuous, surface garbage that encourages flashy, transitory pop fashion and a lust for the latest music/game/device foisted on them by corporations that cleverly disguise themselves as one of them.

Oprah Winfrey asked young girls in America what they wanted most when she was choosing a site to invest millions of dollars in a special school. Their answer? Nike footwear and iPods. The same question put to a group of girls in South Africa brought this response: Education, clean clothes, a chance to better themselves and help others. Guess who got the school?

While we watch shows about wealthy individuals, we are shown advertisements telling us to buy, buy, buy. President George W. Bush famously told Americans to go out and shop after the terrorist attacks of September 11, 2001. He was telling us, essentially, that if we didn't go shopping the terrorists would win, which sounds ridiculous, but he was right! He and economists everywhere knew that the worst thing that could happen after the attacks would be for Americans to stop shopping. If we stopped buying things it would ruin the economy, which would do more harm than the terrorists.

What a silly trap we have stepped in. As Raj Patel said, "We will need to understand that our collective and individual happiness is only damaged by becoming [Allen] Greenspan's monsters, the role for which most of us have been groomed since birth, christened in consumer culture and loaded with material desire until we die." In 1929, just before the other big financial crash, General Motors researcher and inventor Charles Kettering said: "The key to economic prosperity is the organized creation of dissatisfaction."

Our national well-being absolutely depends on mindless consumerism. If Americans don't continue to use their cash and credit cards to buy things they don't need, sales will go down and companies will have to lay off employees who will then not have money to buy anything, driving sales down more. More people will be laid off and not have money to spend, creating an out-of-control spiraling descent. There's precious little breathing room in this system. It's either full steam ahead or panic and crash. It's a circular trap. If we don't keep spending we'll crash now; if we do, we'll all crash later. Either way we'll crash. Using our built-in short-term thinking and decision skills, we always choose later.

We got a big taste of this in late 2008 when years of deceitful and dangerously speculative financial practices succumbed to the inevitable and the western economy came within a hair's breadth of total collapse. We were saved by hundreds of billions of taxpayer dollars being thrown at the very institutions that caused the crisis. We were told that as much as we hated doing it, if we didn't, things would be catastrophically worse. Then we got to enjoy the annual year-end reports from these same corporations that had destroyed the economy as they gave themselves bonuses in the tens of millions of dollars. These people were not creating wealth. They had turned Wall Street into one big casino, casting bets with other peoples' money.

In the movie *Trading Places*, Eddie Murphy played a down-and-out homeless man brought into a large investment firm on a bet over whether a regular guy could do what wealthy investors do. In one scene, they sat him down to explain commodities trading. After explaining, they asked if he understood. He grinned and answered, "Yeah, you two sound like a couple of bookies!"

The upside to the financial crisis of 2008 was that millions of people found themselves questioning their lifestyles, habits and values. Hey, they said, maybe more isn't always better. As millions lost their jobs, people lost the ability to control their debt and maintain high credit scores. Presented with the fact that they couldn't do anything about it, millions stopped trying to maintain their credit score.

A groundswell of introspection swept across the land, and many people began turning the economic disaster into an opportunity to rethink what things in their lives truly had value in the long run. Businesses that sold things people didn't need—and that included a lot of businesses—felt the effects immediately. People stopped buying impulsively and sales plummeted. Some people, feeling they had no alternative, used their credit cards for groceries and utilities. They couldn't pay their credit card bills anymore no matter what they did, so they stopped feeling bad about it. This was about survival. Go ahead, repossess the car, it'll be one less thing to worry about. Of course, after they repossess your car or you fall behind in your credit card payments, your credit score is shot. When your credit score is shot, there's no reason to kill yourself worrying about it, is there?

People who had been sold bad, predatory loans, or used their homes as huge ATM machines found themselves owing more than their houses were worth. Having already ruined their credit scores, they began to walk away from their homes, realizing they were throwing good money after bad. Much criticism has been aimed at homeowners who did this, exposing a long-running double standard. Homeowners who decided that there was no reason to continue paying a loan that could never be paid off were called deadbeats, though large corporations have done this for years. Of course when corporations do this they're not deadbeats, they have shown shrewd business acumen by executing a "strategic default." Donald Trump has done this several times.

When consumers began rethinking the whole debt issue, big corporations had a problem, because people who no longer feared lousy credit scores and no longer feared losing their belongings are like a populace that no longer fears their dictator. Suddenly the power shifts.

Soon after the economy crashed in 2008, large lots full of cars or boats or RVs, with huge banners advertising "Repossessions!" appeared. I pondered the quandary lenders were facing. Each of these repossessions represented someone who had defaulted on a loan, ruined their credit score and took themselves out of the pool of potential consumers. With each repossession these companies grew the pool of non-consumers who no longer qualified to buy another boat or RV because of bad credit. Their loans defaulted as their customer base shrank. The only way the old system would work is if corporate America could keep a robust fear of bad credit scores in the minds of consumers and keep them buying. As soon as people stopped being afraid, the entire system began to unravel.

After the financial crash volunteerism skyrocketed as people with time on their hands and new priorities sought to live on a higher level of community consciousness and give something back. Many people started small businesses, or teamed up to create community collectives. Many credit cards were ritually cut up with the kitchen scissors. Thousands thought about downsizing in a positive, exciting way. People realized that they didn't need such large homes, large car payments or large, expansive lifestyles.

Politicians, including the president, lined up to present ideas to "bring home values back up to where they were before," and "grow the economy," but the overinflated value of homes was a huge part of the problem that caused the crash. Why would we want to work to make that happen again?

The entire economy was built as a house of cards with overpriced stocks and homes, coupled with rampant and irresponsible financial speculation. Like the crash of '29 and the dot.com bubble that burst in the 90s, values were fake, based on nothing but a collective agreement in the minds of the hopeful and the greedy.

There is a prevailing view that when it comes to finances, nothing can go down in value—ever. At some point we came up with the notion that endless financial growth was the only acceptable goal for our country. Not happiness, justice for all or a contented, satisfied population. Our only goal is bigger, larger, MORE. We have always gone forward as a nation with the notion that our country must grow, our influence must grow, our power must grow and our economy must grow forever.

The stock market, driven by greed and fear, occasionally stops and "corrects" itself, which means that values drop to reflect reality. Stocks or houses grow in value to ridiculous amounts, and then the stock or housing market crashes.

Our Gross Domestic Product can never go down or economists panic. This is crazy if you think about it with a long-term perspective. Nothing can grow forever, yet the generally accepted definition of a recession is a decline in the GDP—no matter how slight—for two consecutive quarters. If that happens everybody in Washington blames everybody else, trying to get the fix on the next election. Politicians know that if they espouse anything but endless growth they are out of a job, even though they know it's impossible over the long term. They also know that their constituents—us—usually don't think about the long term, we think about right now. Speaking about any long-term reality is a death knell for elected officials, so they carefully avoid it.

This obsession with growth strips planetary resources faster than they can be replaced, causing untold problems in individual lives, and the tragedy is that it's not making any of us any happier. As Bill McKibben put it: "Since happiness had increased with income in the past, we assumed it would do so in the future...two beers made me feel good, so ten beers will make me feel five times better."

Unfortunately, it doesn't work that way. Endless "more" does not endlessly increase happiness and satisfaction. The General Social Survey (GSS), an organization that monitors social change in the United States with the help of the National Science Foundation, reports that since the 1970s, despite the fact that incomes and home sizes have doubled and our economy has continued to expand, the number of people who identify themselves as being "very happy" has gone down. The study has identified that point where "more" no longer equals "better," which appears to be an income between $50,000 and $75,000 per year. Beyond that, additional income no longer equates to additional happiness.

Yes, more income means you can get more stuff, but apparently it won't do much more than fill up self-storage spaces. It won't make you happier. If, in the words of Kris Kristofferson, "freedom's just another word for nothing left to lose," then having lots to lose must be the antithesis to freedom.

So what will make us happier? We can refer back to those things people name as most important to well-being, things like family, health, love, friendship and peace of mind. This list will be different for each person, but the bottom line is that it will always be a list of those things that remain true over the long run wherever you live in the world, no matter the vagaries of politics, economy or culture.

In a little corner of Asia there is a country that has made happiness a core goal of their culture. The Kingdom of Bhutan, nestled between two powerful giants, India and China, has decided to measure their country's progress not in Gross Domestic Product, but in something they call Gross National Happiness, or GNH. "Happiness is the complete body and mental well-being," said Bhutan's Prime Minister Jigme Thinley in an interview with the New York Times, "and being content with what is and what one has."

Did you flinch when you read that? To western ears a leader telling a population to "be content with what you have," can sound suspiciously like an oppressive regime trying to stifle discontent. After all, here in America we are constantly told to not be content with what we have. We have giant industries built around fomenting discontent so they can sell you something. That's not the case in Bhutan, where they understand long-term thinking. Prime Minister Thinley watched from his mountainous country as America's economy crashed, taking many of the world's economies with it. "Greed," he said, summing up the crisis. "Insatiable human greed." Jigme Thinley may be the leader of a country that is arguably not a significant player on the world stage, and Thinley's explanation was not very sophisticated compared to the hysterical, finger-pointing hyperbole we're used to from our own politicians, but his comment pretty much nailed it.

In 2008 Bhutan's government created a new constitution that requires all proposed government programs—from agriculture, to trade, to transportation—to be vetted not by their economics, but by the amount of happiness they will create. They have even created a well thought out system of measuring happiness that includes the Four Pillars, the Nine Domains and the 72 Indicators of happiness. These are not naïve, backward people playing a game of semantics. They are a people who have eschewed the pitfalls of pursuing happiness by mindless consuming, instead creating conditions that nurture and reward those things that are acknowledged globally to bring contentment and a sense of well-being over the long run.

Yes, it's easier for them to try something like this, with their tiny, difficult-to-reach kingdom and small population. Bhutan is a predominately Buddhist country with a tradition of long-term thinking and spiritual values, but their core ideas are something that can be applied anywhere if we can pull our heads out of the sand, look beyond the short term, and focus on those things that stay true over time. Look at it this way, if I decide not to spend my life frantically racing around in a quest to consume, there's a long-term benefit to the planet by being someone who is helping calm the collective anxiety.

Happily, little Bhutan is not the only country that has begun to realize that measuring progress using only the GDP is woefully inadequate. Great Britain's Prime Minister David Cameron has been promoting a new Happiness Index survey to take the pulse of that country's overall well-being and satisfaction. Prompted partly by a report created by Nobel Prize-winning economists Joseph Stiglitz and Amartya Sen, the United Kingdom has been sending questionnaires to British households asking them to rate their subjective well-being, including a self-rated appraisal of their happiness, and how they feel things are going for them in achieving their life's goals. Both France and Canada are pursuing similar measures. Perhaps it's time that America realized that focusing only on production and consumerism is not an accurate way to understand the well-being of our nation.

Bhutan even has a Secretary for Gross National Happiness. Doesn't that sound like a great job? His name is Karma Tshiteem. "On the personal level," he told the New York Times, "it's about family and friends and having good times to spend with them, and on a professional level it's finding work that gives your life some meaning. We feel that's a worthwhile dream."

Friends, family, the time to enjoy them and meaningful work. Well said indeed. These are the things that bring contentment, fulfillment and happiness to our lives. Intuitively, we all know this. None of this is to say that money, wealth and financial success are inherently bad things. Financial success can bring a sense of freedom and provide options that are otherwise unavailable, but when we forget that money is merely a tool and begin to believe that acquiring things brings us happiness, we create discord in our life. The question arises, I have all these wonderful things, why am I not happy? We already know the answer if we will allow ourselves to step back and take a wider, longer view.

Our economy, the way it is now designed, will not work unless we collectively continue to acquire debt and buy things we don't need. That doesn't mean that any of us as individuals have to participate. Taking the long-term view there is much to be said for downsizing, reducing complications, drama and chaos, and extricating ourselves from the trap of overconsumption and debt.

When enough of us decide to opt out of the never-ending quest for happiness via material things, change will come to our society from within and we will begin, together, to realign our priorities. When that happens we will be happier for it. We can choose, right now, to do things differently.

Do you have the time to enjoy and nurture relationships with friends and family, or are you always racing to the next task in order to "feed the monster?" Do you really need more possessions? Are you enjoying the ones you have? We all need money for shelter and food. We need to take care of our children. But we don't need to destroy our lives in a never-ending uphill battle to increase our possessions. It doesn't enhance our lives and it doesn't make us happy.

Despite what we see and hear each day from the corporate giants that control our country, we don't have to increase our debt and acquire more possessions to be happy. In the long run, we just need to decide that enough is in fact enough, and remember that the best things in life aren't things. I agree with Karma Tshiteem: it's a worthwhile dream.

7

SUSTAINABLE FOOD, SUSTAINABLE FUTURE

Grow the mind to grow the soil to grow the food that strengthens the community.

Tara Smith, owner, Tara Firma Farms

Eat food, not too much, mostly plants.

Michael Pollan

When I was eighteen years old I found my-self in the navy in Tokyo, Japan, standing bewildered on the street, not knowing the language or much else. Though I was a stranger in a strange land, when it came time to eat I felt right at home on that busy Tokyo street. In one sweep of the eyes I saw a McDonald's, Pizza Hut and Kentucky Fried Chicken, all within a hundred yards or so of each other. All fast food options being more or less equal, I chose McDonald's, and ordered from a menu of laminated photographs. The friendly Japanese girl behind the counter helped me as I pointed to the photo of the Big Mac, French fries and so on.

I went all the way to Japan, a culture with a rich culinary tradition, and ate a Big Mac on the street while the culture and citizenry of Tokyo swirled around me. This was typical American behavior. I was a product of my time and my culture. When far away from home we often seek those things that feel less foreign. I grew up eating at McDonald's whenever I could, like most of my peers. I can remember when they used to post the number of hamburgers they had sold on their signs. "Over 20 million served," the sign proclaimed. My friends and I enjoyed watching them raise that number as time went by, knowing that some of those burgers had been "served" to us; we'd done our part. Over time, the "number served" became so huge that they stopped posting it.

That was in 1976. Since then the American fast food industry has had decades to insinuate itself into the rest of the world, effectively homogenizing our planet, making one place much the same as the next. Today you can find McDonald's pretty much everywhere. I read a long time ago that no two countries that had McDonald's restaurants within their borders had ever gone to war with each other. I didn't know quite what to do with that piece of information, but it was strangely comforting. It seems that if a country was stable enough—and in bed with the West enough—to let McDonald's in, they were unlikely to cause trouble while raking in the big bucks by serving those zillions of delicious burgers. McDonald's hamburgers had, for a time, become the great peacemaker.

But not everybody wants a McDonald's next door, or even in town. In 1986, when the ever-expanding McDonald's Corporation planned a new store in the Piazza di Spagna in Rome, Italian citizen and food writer Carlo Petrini became incensed at the prospect of the golden arches encroaching further into his culture. Petrini, already an outspoken critic of "the Americanism" of food in his country, decided that something had to be done to counter this influence. Since in his view fast food was the problem, Petrini founded Slow Food, an organization that encourages us to rediscover and protect our culinary traditions. Petrini drafted a Slow Food manifesto, which three years later was signed by representatives of twenty countries. It's worth reading.

> Our century, which began and has developed under the insignia of industrial civilization, first invented the machine and then took it as its life model.

We are enslaved by speed and have all succumbed to the same insidious virus: Fast Life, which disrupts our habits, pervades the privacy of our homes and forces us to eat Fast Foods.

To be worthy of the name, Homo Sapiens should rid himself of speed before it reduces him to a species in danger of extinction.

A firm defense of quiet material pleasure is the only way to oppose the universal folly of Fast Life.

May suitable doses of guaranteed sensual pleasure and slow, long-lasting enjoyment preserve us from the contagion of the multitude who mistake frenzy for efficiency.

Our defense should begin at the table with Slow Food. Let us rediscover the flavors and savors of regional cooking and banish the degrading effects of Fast Food.

In the name of productivity, Fast Life has changed our way of being and threatens our environment and our landscapes. So Slow Food is now the only truly progressive answer.

> That is what real culture is all about: developing taste rather than demeaning it. And what better way to set about this than an international exchange of experiences, knowledge, projects?
>
> Slow Food guarantees a better future.
>
> Slow Food is an idea that needs plenty of qualified supporters who can help turn this (slow) motion into an international movement, with the little snail as its symbol.

The Slow Food movement, whose logo is a snail—the slowest food—grew, and today boasts over 100,000 members with chapters they call conviviums all over the world. There is more to the Slow Food movement than good meals. They embrace a long-term outlook when it comes to what we eat, and they are seeking to preserve endangered foods. According to Slow Food literature, fast food culture and the advent of so many processed foods has threatened some traditional foods with extinction. The Slow Food movement encourages people to seek out and consume these foods as a way to preserve the culinary traditions of cultures around the world and in our own backyards. The movement also teaches stewardship of the land, ecologically sound food production and cultural diversity.

The advent of fast food changed everything. It can be traced back to the original McDonald's, started in 1940 by brothers Richard and Maurice McDonald in San Bernardino, California.

The brothers McDonald developed what they called the Speedee Service System, laying the foundation for the fast-food systems throughout the world in tens of thousands of fast-food outlets. Their original sign read "McDonald's Famous Hamburgers: Buy 'em by the bag." The price for a hamburger was fifteen cents.

Their new system of efficient methods of preparing hamburgers, french fries and milk shakes caught the attention of entrepreneur Ray Croc. Croc had been a paper-cup salesman, a jazz musician and a salesman of new multi-mixer milkshake machines that were just appearing at the time. The McDonald brothers had purchased eight of those machines from Croc. It occurred to him that as the McDonald brothers opened new stores, he could sell more in each new location. He ended up purchasing his own McDonald's franchise in 1955, and eventually became the company's franchising agent, in charge of expanding the outlets and creating even more efficient ways of delivering burgers and fries in a speedy manner.

Ray Croc had larger eyes than the McDonald brothers. Over time he grew frustrated with their willingness to accept slow growth, and their satisfaction with only having several stores. In 1961 he purchased the company outright from the brothers, except for the original store, and set about creating the behemoth that we all know today. Ray Croc purchased the rights to the name, and forced the McDonald brothers to change the name of their original restaurant to "Big M," which doesn't quite have the same ring, does it?

Croc immediately instigated changes throughout his new company. Borrowing from the legendary assembly line mentality of car moguls Henry Ford and Ransom Eli Olds, he instituted a strict policy of standardization and mechanization in each restaurant with rigid guidelines for food preparation and presentation. He wanted to create consistency in the minds of his customers, so that as the franchise expanded they would come to know that a McDonald's hamburger or french fries would look and taste the same no matter where a person encountered one. It worked. When I ate my Big Mac on the bustling streets of Tokyo in 1976, it looked and tasted just like the ones I used to buy in Southern California. McDonald's became listed on the stock exchange in 1965, Croc became fabulously wealthy, and the rest is history.

Many other fast food chains appeared. Wendy's, Jack-in-the-Box, White Castle, Burger King, Carl's Jr.—the age of the drive-through was upon us.

The rise of the fast-food restaurant quickly led to a fundamental change in the way we eat and produce food in America. Demand for those things fast-food restaurants require—beef, potatoes, lettuce, tomatoes, bread, pickles, bacon, and chicken—led to a huge ramping up of production on our farms. Not only did all those restaurants demand more of these things, they wanted them to look and taste a specific way. They needed consistency and they needed it fast. This demand had a lot to do with creating today's industrialized food system, which has one goal: bigger, faster profits. Forget the iconic mom and pop farm with its red barn, pastoral setting and hoedowns on the weekends. For the past 50 or 60 years those farms have been steadily disappearing from the landscape. According to the United States Department of Agriculture (USDA), from 1950 to 2003 the number of farms in the United States shrank from 5,382,162, to 2,121,107, a difference of over three and a quarter million.

In their place an ever-smaller number of mega-corporations have taken over an ever-larger portion of the food industry. These industrial giants control what is grown, where it's grown, how it's grown and how it's distributed. To answer the double demands of consistent, fast-growing food and a growing population, food production in America has become as mechanized as any other assembly-line system. Growers have succeeded wonderfully from a business standpoint, but not from a human, animal or ecological standpoint.

We have changed much from the archetypal agrarian people we once were. Fewer and fewer of us farm anymore. For many Americans any direct connection to the source of our food has been effectively severed. Ask a typical kid where beef or apples or any food comes from. They often answer, from the grocery store, of course! (The same way that money comes from the ATM.) Why would they believe any differently? Many of them have never seen a farm except in a television ad. In the long run it would serve all of us well to pay more attention to where our food comes from, because the model we're using now to grow and distribute our food not only has direct negative effects on our personal health, it affects the well-being of our entire planet.

In America we are used to cheap, affordable food. We expect it and for the most part we get it. As a nation we spend an average of nine to 10 percent of our income on food. In the 1930s, it was common to spend as much as a quarter of our income on food. Our food today is really cheap. You can get a hamburger at most fast-food places for a dollar. How is this even possible? Looking at the system through the filter of long-term thinking, we ask again: Is it sustainable? For a multitude of reasons, the answer is no. We have created a way to produce massive amounts of food for a low cost at the cash register, but in so doing we have foisted most of the "true costs" of those foods onto the environment and our health.

When the mega farming businesses began snapping up small farms across America, to "grow" our beef or chicken, efficiency became the watchword. If they needed more product they had to figure out how to best maximize return and minimize costs. Over the years this has led to huge, inhumane facilities where animals are crammed together in nightmarish conditions. The industry term for these places is CAFO, which sounds like some sort of coffee drink but is an acronym meaning Concentrated Animal Feeding Operation, though some call them nightmare factories.

At the CAFOs cattle are crammed side by side in small holding cells, where the only goal is to fatten them up the most in the shortest period of time. To do this, the cattle are injected with growth hormones to make them grow larger and faster than normal in the cramped conditions in which they live their miserable lives. They are not allowed to engage in normal cattle behavior, which keeps them perpetually under stress and fear until they are slaughtered. There is no grass, no open spaces and no place to get away. Numb, stressed, artificially fattened and out of their minds, they are then slaughtered and turned into dollar burgers.

Chicken farms often raise literally hundreds of thousands of birds in giant, dark, closed, windowless spaces, with chickens stacked in cages on top of each other so that waste from the higher birds falls on the chickens below. These birds never see daylight their entire lives. Because Americans like white chicken breast meat, some of these chickens have been bred to produce artificially large breasts. Some are so out of proportion that the birds can only walk a couple of steps before collapsing from the weight of their breasts and the weakness of their legs. Not a lot of care is given because the company knows they are there on a very temporary basis. Soon, they will become chicken nuggets. Sometimes their beaks are cut off to prevent them from pecking at each other from stress. These of conditions hold true for pig and turkey factories as well. It's something the corporations don't want you to see, and for most people it's something we don't want to see. This system has allowed corporate factories to crank out billions of pounds of protein at very low cost.

And that's what we want, right? Low cost? Isn't that the bottom line in every purchase? Every family that struggles to put food on the table likes the idea of food that is affordable and plentiful. The problem is that as in so many other industries, the true cost of what we are buying is hidden from view.

The Sierra Club National Sustainable Consumption Committee began a program titled The True Cost of Food in 2003.

According to their research, when all of the other costs are added your steak should cost around $815 per pound. Growing beef requires at least one gallon of oil and 2500 pounds of water per pound of meat. It also takes 10 pounds of corn or grain to provide one pound of meat. Meanwhile we're experiencing large-scale global destruction of forests and grassland to grow the food for cattle, which is ironic when you think about it, because cows are designed to eat grass. In a video produced by the Sierra Club they highlight the fact that "cows crap about 60 pounds per day," or about 12 tons per year. Even a small feedlot can produce more waste than a city of 25,000 people. Small family farms can recycle this waste, as they have enough space for each cow to graze naturally, preventing over grazing and fertilizing the land in a sustainable way.

Factory farms, which cram as many animals together as possible, create 291 billion tons of cow manure per year, which causes huge pollution problems in our rivers and drinking supplies. Our obsession with beef helps create air pollution as the collective farts of all those unhappy cows produce over 180 billion cubic feet of methane gas, contributing to global warming.

Because CAFOs are raising animals in unhealthy environments they have to continually stuff them with antibiotics to stave off illness, which would be rampant under those conditions without them. These antibiotics are passed on to us when we eat the meat. If you eat factory-farmed meat your body is exposed to antibiotics on a grand scale. Over exposure to antibiotics helps create super strains of bacteria. You can never kill them all and the survivors pass on their immunity to the next generations. The industry has to constantly play catch up by creating new antibiotics to stay ahead of nature.

In order to increase profits by shortening the time it takes an animal to mature and add extra, unnatural weight, cows, pigs and chickens are fed artificial growth hormones that are also passed on to you, the consumer. In those cramped conditions, disease can spread quickly. Since the "farmer" doesn't know the animals personally, sick cows are not always identified, in contrast to small family farm operations where a sick cow that's not acting right is easily spotted. In the end, all the cows are slaughtered together and their meat is mixed and mingled. A sick cow's meat taints all the rest, and then someone buys it at a drive-through and feeds it to their kids. While it does represent good profits and cheap food, none of this represents good long-term thinking.

In the Midwest, one can drive for miles and miles past identical rows of corn or wheat. Millions of acres are often devoted to only one crop. There is no room for diversity or balance and no room for anything other than the most cash-intensive crops, heavily subsidized by taxpayer dollars. With no natural diversity and no variation among the crops, the plants are scarily susceptible to disease or pests.

When every plant is the same it only takes one bug or disease to end it all. In nature there is not only a variety of plants growing in any one place, but plenty of variation among the individual plants of each species. This variation is necessary for a healthy environment. If a pest comes along, and there is always a new one, the variation among the plants enables them to survive. One particular plant may succumb, but the population will have enough genetic variation to ward off the threat so every single plant doesn't die. In today's yield-intensive agricultural growing model, those problems are addressed by fighting nature with modern chemical pesticides.

Apples are a great example of modern monoculture. Wild apple trees produce a wide variety of apples from seeds from the same tree. If you plant a seed from, say, a golden delicious apple, you will not get a golden delicious apple tree. The new tree will produce an entirely different, random type of apple. The scientific term for this is heterozygote, which is an organism that does not produce offspring similar to the parents. In order to get the uniformity that we have come to expect, apple trees must be "cloned." We take grafts from existing trees and turn them into large orchards of what are, in effect, the same trees. This is the only way to consistently get the same types of apples.

Because our apple orchards consist of grafts of the same tree, they have no diversity and are particularly vulnerable to disease or pests. With little or no variation, one unexpected disease or pest can ruin the entire crop. For this reason, apples are among the top recipients of massive doses of pesticides. We get uniform apples of the same shape and color, but we pay for this by poisoning the food we eat.

In America we douse our crops with a billion pounds of pesticides every year. These pesticides don't just kill the "pests," they kill the good bugs as well. The problem is that each time you douse a field with a new pesticide you kill most, but not all of the bugs. Some are naturally immune. Those that live reproduce and the next generation shares their immunity to that chemical. Modern farming is a never ending race to create new versions of pesticides.

These pesticides also kill the soil itself. Soil is not just dirt; it is a living, breathing thing, comprised of decomposed bodies of plants, insects, animals and billions of living bacteria, all of which combine to nourish the plants that grow in it. When over farming and excessive chemical use renders it sterile and bare, our only alternative is to move to another place or replace the lost nutrients with artificial fertilizers and chemicals. Those fertilizers and chemicals soak into our ground water and run off the land during rains and floods, contaminating our rivers and oceans while lacing our drinking water with poison. According to the Environmental Protection Agency, we could save 15 billion dollars in water treatment plants if we cut agricultural toxins.

Let's stop and consider that last statement for a moment. Does it seem strange to anyone else that we so casually put the words "agricultural" and "toxins" together? As though "agricultural toxins" were a normal thing? According to the Sierra Club, in the 1930s, before the onset of the widespread use of pesticides, the United States lost approximately 30 percent of its wheat crop to bugs. In 2000, after pouring tens of millions of tons of poison on our wheat crops, we lose 37 percent of our wheat to bugs. Despite all our best efforts at controlling nature through chemicals and poisons, we are losing seven percent more than before we began using them.

Modern agribusiness has trapped itself in an unsustainable model of using artificial fertilizers, chemicals and pesticides to battle pests and keep the soil producing. It is a battle they are slowly losing. All of these substances are heavily dependent on fossil fuels. We have come up with a way to grow massive amounts of food with few workers, but we have become dependent on oil to do much of the work. According to author and environmentalist Richard Manning, "All together the food-processing industry in the United States uses about ten calories of fossil fuel for every calorie of food energy it produces."

We also are using massive amounts of energy to transport our crops. With the advent of mega agribusiness and the subsequent decline of family owned farms, much of the food we consume is produced somewhere far away, and then driven to your local store. The average American meal has traveled 1500 to 2000 miles to your plate. When you buy locally produced foods, the average trip is about 55 miles. An oft-repeated quote illustrating this problem comes from ecological economist Herman Daly, who observed that America exports sugar cookies to Holland, and Holland exports sugar cookies to America. Exclaimed Daly, "Exchanging recipes would surely be more efficient."

Today just seven percent of farms sell 72 percent of all food grown in America and that seven percent is heavily reliant on oil. Even a little unrest in the Middle East can translate to a catastrophe in food production. Writer and environmentalist Bill Mckibben said, "Because of its reliance on cheap energy, the efficiency of our vast farms and the food system they underwrite is in one sense an illusion, and perhaps a very temporary one."

Higher yields, more food, lower prices, the wonders of modern agriculture. Most of us, in the frantic busyness of our everyday lives, don't allocate much time to ponder this. We dash to the supermarket to grab something for dinner and that's the end of it. We are not encouraged to look too closely at how things are done. But we need to step back and take a long, hard look at this system, and the laws put in place to support it.

Though many of us have come to see eating as just one more task to do during the day, to be done as quickly, efficiently and cheaply as possible, the food we eat is perhaps the most basic foundation of our day-to-day life. It contributes to the health or disease of our bodies; it connects us intimately with the Earth we depend on. When we bite into an apple or a steak or a trout we are sinking our teeth into billions of years of evolution, taking part in the oldest symbiotic relationship there is: the cycle of sunlight, soil and the endless energy loops that bind our planet and all its living inhabitants together. When we eat anything we are literally eating the Earth, running a small part of our miraculous, unlikely planet through our body, gleaning energy gifted from the sun, wrought through plants by the miracle of photosynthesis, then through animals that acquire their energy from the plants, each tuned perfectly over millions of years to play their part in the eternal energy cycle.

Refrigerated supermarket shelves, food dyes, plastic bags and vacuum-sealed meats aside, we are not separate from this system, we are smack in the middle of it. It is in our best interest to take part consciously with a commitment to the health of the whole. Healthy food, in my opinion, falls under the auspices of the commons, like clean air or water. It is a right and a need of every living being. When we allow something as elemental as our food to be placed under the purview of the corporate profit motive, we have ceded not only our direct access to food grown naturally with our physical well-being in mind, we have relinquished a part of our humanity and our innate connection to the planet that has evolved beautifully over billions of years to sustain us.

I'm not saying that it's wrong to grow a crop of animals or vegetables and sell them for a profit. But what has happened to our system of food production goes well beyond simply making a profit. We have allowed corporations so much control over what is grown, how it's grown and who can to grow it that we have put our health and that of our planet in the hands of companies that value profits over health, and rising quarterly reports over ecological stewardship. The corporations are making fat profits and providing cheap food, but the ecological and health damage is being borne by everyone else. Author Raj Patel, said, "This is why food grown through industrial agriculture, which doesn't pay the full price of its ecological misbehavior, appears cheaper at the supermarket checkout. What the hidden costs show is that this is not cheap food, it's cheat food."

In 1978 a man named Ananda Mohan Chakrabarty, who worked for General Electric, developed, through genetic engineering, a new form of bacteria never seen before on Earth, and applied for a patent. The bacteria in question were designed to "eat" oil and help clean up oil spills. A question quickly arose. Could a person patent a living thing? This was unprecedented. Chakrabarty's patent was denied initially because it was generally accepted at that time that patent law did not apply to living organisms. He appealed and the United States Court of Customs and Patent Appeals overturned the original decision, stating that "...the fact that micro-organisms are alive is without legal significance for purposes of patent law."

The Patent and Trademark office appealed that decision, and in 1980 the Supreme Court decided the case in Chakrabarty's favor in a 5 to 4 decision. The Supremes decided that: "A live, human-made micro-organism is patentable subject matter under [Title 35 U.S. C.] 101. Respondent's micro-organism constitutes a 'manufacture' or 'composition of matter' within that statute."

That decision slipped under radar for most of us. But we should take notice because the Supreme Court ruling rendered that day changed the whole game. You can patent life? Without a vote by congress or the public, a decision was made that profoundly changed the way corporations and agribusiness went about planning the future of the food we eat, affecting your future and mine.

That future was rosy for those companies that could take advantage of the new rules. Monsanto in particular began a program of developing and patenting genetically modified plants and seeds. Today they hold the patents to over 11,000 seeds, many of which our nation and much of the world depend on for sustenance. Farmers wanting to grow the corn, or soybeans, or wheat or whatever that springs from those seeds are beholden to Monsanto for their livelihood. Since Monsanto owns the "rights" to the use of these seeds, it illegal for farmers to grow these crops without paying hefty fees to Monsanto and farmers are prohibited from saving seeds from this year's crop to start next year's—a basic tenet of farming since the advent of agriculture some 10,000 years ago. If they try to save seeds they can—and will—be sued by Monsanto's well-funded legal team. To preclude this from happening in the first place, the clever genetic engineers at Monsanto actually began experimenting with crop seeds that had built-in "suicide genes," that caused these crops to become sterile after one planting, but they later dropped this program.

There has been much controversy over genetically engineered foods, sometimes called "frankenfoods." The companies doing the engineering argue that the modifications have enabled farmers to produce much greater yields at lower costs, since many of the modifications have to do with resistance to pests or weeds. Bright people have argued that there is nothing to worry about; humans have been genetically modifying plants and animals for thousands of years. Every breed of cow, every crop we grow, every type of dog or cat we have as pets have been altered through crossing different plants or animals over time, encouraging those traits we like and discouraging those we don't, and this too is genetic engineering, strictly speaking.

But what today's corporations are doing in laboratories is altering the genetic blueprint of plants in a controlled environment, forcing certain desirable, profitable traits into the mix, then letting them loose in the world where those traits can potentially be passed on to other plants with unknown consequences. Many of the genetic modifications have to do with resistance to these companies' own herbicides.

For example, Monsanto is the maker of a weed killer known as Roundup, a product used by home gardeners to help keep weeds down. Huge farms, like small gardeners, have to deal with unwanted weeds, but they can't spray weed killer over all the crops because it will also kill the crops. To solve this, Monsanto genetically engineered their crop seeds to be what they call "Roundup ready," meaning Roundup won't kill them. Now, ostensibly, the farmers can spray everything with Roundup and only the weeds will die, leaving the crops unscathed. Monsanto claims it is safe, but recent disturbing evidence has revealed that Roundup is responsible for birth defects in animals and possibly humans.

Other genetic modifications have to do with altering size or color to make the produce more supermarket friendly, more appealing to the eye. Flavor and nutrition are not the priorities. It's about volume and aesthetics. People often say that the tomatoes they get in the stores today, while large, ruby red, and juicy, don't have anywhere near the flavor they remember from homegrown varieties they used to eat. The argument over whether we should or shouldn't produce genetically modified foods has largely become moot. Today, around 78 percent of food sold in our major supermarkets contains genetically modified ingredients.

All of the poisonous chemicals that are sprayed on crops designed to resist them are absorbed into those plants, and we ingest these poisons at the dinner table. There are always some weeds that don't die from being bathed in Roundup, leaving them to reproduce and create resistant strains. This requires new formulations of the herbicide to keep up with natural selection, then more genetic modifications to the plant in order to keep up.

Thus we again find ourselves in something like an arms race: one side creates an effective weapon and the other side comes up with a counter to that weapon, so the first side creates a bigger, better weapon. That inspires the other side to create a new deterrent, and so on. But this is our food we're talking about. We shouldn't be taking up arms against nature because we are a part of nature, and nature always wins those fights in the long run. Finally, it hurts farmers who aren't using Roundup ready plants. Behold Monsanto's audacity.

In 1997, Percy Schmeiser, a 68-year-old Canadian canola farmer who managed a 1400 acre spread got an unexpected visit from a corporate behemoth. Percy describes himself as a "seed developer" and "seed saver." During a half-century of expert husbandry Percy had carefully nurtured his crops, gently nudging them by careful seed selection, to produce a healthy canola crop that thrived in that environment. He wasn't interested in the new laboratory produced, genetically modified seeds that were becoming the norm on many farms, but without Percy's knowledge a neighboring farmer had planted a field of genetically modified canola plants near his farm.

One day, representatives of Monsanto Corporation obtained samples of Percy's canola plants and found that his crop contained Monsanto's patented genetically altered strain of canola, so the company sued him for patent infringement, though he had never planted their version of the crop, used their seeds or done anything to get their patented genetic material into his crops. Monsanto claimed that Percy owed them licensing fees, arguing that since they own the rights to the genetically altered seeds they have the right to control their use, including saving seeds for next year's crop. Farmers that use Monsanto's seeds have a contractual agreement to not save seeds, and have to buy new seeds from Monsanto each year. Percy said his right to own and save seeds from his crop took precedence over Monsanto's claims, and it was an accident that the canola entered his fields by natural methods like breezes and insects. Monsanto said he did it on purpose. The issue was settled in Monsanto's favor by the Federal Court of Canada. A stunned Percy summed it up after the decision, "Regardless of how genetically altered canola gets on a person's land, it's the property of Monsanto."

This travesty is by no means an isolated case. Monsanto has filed over 2000 similar lawsuits against farmers around the world. Monsanto and other companies that produce chemicals, pesticides and petroleum-based fertilizers have bought many of the seed companies, giving them virtual autonomy over food production and control over farmers.

And just in case you still think companies like Monsanto are looking out for your best interests, Phil Angell, Director of Corporate Communications for Monsanto in 1998, summed up his company's viewpoint this way: "Monsanto should not have to vouchsafe the safety of biotech foods. Our interest is in selling as much of it as possible. Assuring its safety is the FDA's job."

The problem is that various presidents have appointed former Monsanto executives to FDA positions overseeing their old industry. We have literally put the foxes in charge of the hen house. Monsanto isn't the only company producing genetically modified foods and taking patents out on seeds. There are several, all looking to increase profits on the backs of the environment and our future, often combining their efforts across a swath of interests. The largest genetically modified food manufacturers also own the largest pharmaceutical and pesticide companies. The good news is that groups of farmers have banded together and have been allowed to sue Monsanto for "contaminating" their crops with genetically modified plants.

These mega-corporations have deep pockets and plenty of lobbyists making large cash donations to ensure that lawmakers do their bidding and keep huge taxpayer subsidies coming their way. In 2006 taxpayers paid out $56.2 billion in federal corn subsidies, which is why corn is over produced and is an ingredient in nearly every processed food, as are soybeans, another heavily subsidized crop. Both are used as cattle feed because they're cheap, even though cattle are not designed to eat corn and it is unhealthy for them to do so. But it does help fatten them up more quickly.

The industry doesn't stop there. Since the early 1990s agribusiness lobbyists have managed to push laws through at least a dozen state legislatures that prohibit "disparagement" of agriculture. These laws, sometimes called "banana bills" or "veggie libel" laws, allow food producers to sue people who publically state anything bad about the industry. Traditionally, to be found guilty of libel what you say has to be false, but a bill put forth in Illinois wants you to be prosecuted for saying anything that "tends to lower the agricultural producer or product in the estimation of the community." Oprah Winfrey was sued under one of these laws after she aired a television show in which she said something about meat that the beef industry didn't like.

In addition, there have been attempts to pass laws prohibiting the taking of photos or videos at "farm facilities." These "ag gag" bills arose because of the furor over secret footage released on the Internet showing the inhumane conditions at some beef-producing CAFOs. If passed these laws would also prohibit anyone from publishing or showing these photos or videos, which means it would be illegal for a news organization to air them.

Clearly, the food industry does not want you thinking about any of this, or taking a closer look. They know that the more informed consumers are about how their food is produced the more likely they are to ask questions. Joel Salatin, owner of Polyface Farms in Virginia, talked about this in the movie Food, Inc. "The industrial food system gradually became so noisy, smelly—not a person-friendly place, that the people who operate these plants don't want anybody to go there, because then people would see the ugly truth. When that occurred we lost all the integrity, all the accountability in the food system."

The FDA continues to approve such products as recombinant bovine growth hormone and genetically-modified tomatoes while food safety and environmental groups keep crying foul. The food producing and processing industries have even lobbied intensively to keep from having to label genetically modified foods as being genetically modified, an attempt to keep you in the dark about something potentially harmful or something you might think twice about if you had the information.

Since the advent of the mega farm as a model for food production, varieties of crops have diminished at an astounding rate. Because of the need for consistency in fast food, or a certain color or size of fruit in the grocery store that is easier to produce on a mass scale, most of the world is dependent on just a few crops—three actually—corn, wheat, and rice. As agribusiness becomes more efficient, larger and more in control, we are playing Russian roulette with our food supply by altering our ecosystems to benefit two or three species to the exclusion of all others, a practice known as monoculture or homogeneity. According to Edward O. Wilson, "The world's food supply hangs by a slender thread of biodiversity. Twenty species carry most of the load, of whom only three—wheat, maize and rice—stand between humanity and starvation."

In an article for YES! magazine Winona LaDuke pointed out that in Canada three-quarters of all the crop varieties that existed before the 20th century are extinct. Of the remaining 25 percent, only 10 percent are available commercially from Canadian seed companies. As we've seen, less diversity means more vulnerability to something unexpected, like diseases or pests that mutate and take out a large part of our food supply. Food writer Michael Pollan summed it up this way: "The bottom line is that industrial food production is largely a lie. The costs are not honest, the production is not honest, the processing is not honest."

And there you are. We've ended up with a food production model that hurts our environment, damages our health and gives control over a basic human need to the quest for increased profit. It's not even good for us. Our Western diet is so laden with sugar, fat, pesticides and additives that obesity, diabetes and cancer are rampant.

So where do we go from here? Is it possible to feed such a large a population another way? Many scientists and environmentalists say yes. In fact, a group of leading scientists, farmers and economists published a paper in the journal Science that called for a dramatic shift in the policies our government puts forth in this area, asking for policies that are "more economically, socially, and environmentally sustainable." The paper, Toward Sustainable Agricultural Systems in the 21st Century, goes on to say that, "We have the technology and the science right now to grow food in sustainable ways, but we lack the policies and markets to make it happen." It pointed out that by introducing more organic farming and grass-fed productions into agriculture and by changing policy incentives, the nation's agricultural system would be better equipped to deal with several environmental impacts such as climate change, biodiversity loss and resource issues.

If we leave these decisions to the government and the marketplace, nothing will change any time soon, but together we make changes that will benefit not only our personal lives, but also the lives of our communities and our planet. It's a matter of looking at it through the lens of long-term thinking. Here are a few questions to ponder:

In the long run…

Is it okay that companies are allowed to genetically alter or irradiate food in ways that may have deleterious effects on our health?

Is it okay that in order to satiate our love of meat, companies are allowed to raise animals in inhumane conditions bordering on torture while filling them with growth hormones and antibiotics, which are passed to us and our children in our food?

Is it okay that the farming methods in wide use today are degrading our environment at an alarming pace and making our food security vulnerable to the ups and downs of the oil market?

Is it okay for companies to patent and own seeds and control what is grown and how it's grown, while suing small farmers who don't toe the line?

Is it okay that we are losing thousands of natural varieties of foods so we can farm only those few that have been determined to be the most profitable?

Is it okay that our processed foods are filled with additives, stuffed with fat and sugars that contribute to diabetes and obesity on a grand scale?

Is it okay that taxpayer dollars subsidize all of this, emphasizing a few grain crops used mainly for animal feed and processed food?

Is it okay that this system drains our aquifers, destroys the soil, and pollutes the environment?

These are questions we should be asking. Let's look at some alternatives that can be easily incorporated into most of our daily lives and that will put us on the path of being less of the problem, and more of the solution. We'll start with a large example, and then narrow it down to your neighborhood.

In 1989, when the Soviet Union finally threw in the towel and the Berlin wall came down, there was celebrating all around the world—except in Cuba, where the collapse of the Soviet Union was looked on with grave misgivings. For nearly thirty years the Soviet Union had been Cuba's benefactor, sending them all manner of materials, subsidies, food, seeds, oil, weapons and everything else they needed to keep functioning. With the collapse of the Soviets, Cuba was in the position of a remittance man getting a letter from his dad saying, sorry, the money's run out. You're on your own.

The Cuban's refer to that scary time as the "Special Period." Through the auspices of the Soviets, Cuban food production at that time was heavily industrialized with large infusions of artificial fertilizers, pesticides and mechanized farming techniques provided by their communist sugar daddy. When the

Soviets collapsed, Cuba lost upwards of 50 percent of their oil imports, 85 percent of its trade economy and much of the taken-for-granted things that kept life humming and food on the table. Their farms collapsed, their transport systems fell by the wayside and the entire nation found itself facing a serious food crisis. This, coupled with the 30-year-old American trade embargo, which remains in place to this day, put them in dire straits.

The United Nation's Food and Agriculture food balance sheets revealed that from 1989 to 1993 the number of food calories available to the average Cuban dropped from 3,012 to 2,325, leading to an average weight loss of 20 pounds per person. Faced with worsening food availability, Cubans were forced to become innovative, self-reliant and resourceful, or starve.

They stepped up to the plate and began a nationwide program of organic farming. Empty plots in Havana and other major cities were converted to community gardens. In the countryside they stopped growing as much sugar, which they used to sell at a handsome profit to the Soviets, and began planting a wide variety of food crops. Since they didn't have access to the pesticides and artificial fertilizers they depended upon in the past, they were forced to find a way to farm organically. Synthetic fertilizers were replaced by animal waste and organic compost. Diverse crop farming using insect and other natural pest control methods, such as spraying with tobacco juice, replaced large monoculture systems. Machines were replaced with humans and animals, and every available plot was put to use to grow food.

Cuban citizens, who used to have other careers as engineers or factory workers, found themselves overseeing organic community gardens. The Cubans didn't see this as an experiment; they saw it as integral to their security and viability as a nation. After a visit to Cuba, writer Roger Doiron observed, "When you visit Havana and you see its crumbling colonial buildings and vintage cars, you can't help feel a bit like a time traveler, but when it comes to sustainable urban agriculture however, a trip to Havana may well be a trip to the future." Cuba's system is not perfect, and they still import some foods, but they rose to the crisis and continue to improve on a successful foray into organic, local, sustainable agriculture on a national level. Calorie counts are back up and they no longer face starvation.

Many are following their lead here in the United States. They practice agroecology, which is a system of applying ecological principles to the production of food, fiber or other growing things. Across the country there are thousands of smaller organic and sustainable farms raising grass-fed beef and free-range chickens, as well as growing crops without daily infusions of poisons.

The rise of organic markets across the U.S. shows a demand for healthier, more sustainably grown food. Farmers' markets can now be found in nearly every community in America, and are the fastest growing food distribution system in the country today. The food sold at farmers' markets tends to be seasonal, fresh, pesticide free and local. The money earned goes into the pockets of local farmers and is then circulated in their local communities.

Many small farms have begun something called Community Supported Agriculture (CSA). CSA programs offer fresh, organic, locally grown foods to customers, who sign up for weekly or monthly deliveries. These deliveries often include a variety of meats or vegetables, depending on what is being produced on the farm that time of year, so it varies as the seasons change. It's a win-win situation. The buyers get nothing but the best and freshest foods available in their local area and the farmers get a steady, dependable customer base.

Recently I took a trip to a local, organic farm near my home. Tara Firma Farms, located in the rolling green hills of Petaluma in Sonoma County, produces vegetables, beef, pork and chicken that it sells to enthusiastic customers around the county. Owned by Tara Smith, a long-term thinker who had a career in the corporate world for much of her adult life, Tara Firma Farms represents all that can go right with food production. Tara and I, along with her dog, Roland, and two goats that apparently think they're dogs too, took a walk around her farm. Along the way she pointed out vegetable gardens, lush and green with the latest seasonal delights, and all grown pesticide free. Baby chickens enjoyed their day in large, open-bottomed cages that kept them safe from predators. The cages are moved each day so the chickens continuously visit fresh areas with new bugs to eat, and are able to naturally fertilize entire meadows over time with their droppings. Her beef cows and pigs are also moved to new areas for the same reason. Nothing is overgrazed and everything is allowed to recover and rejuvenate as the animals move on. Though ultimately slated to be turned into food, these animals are living happy, stress-free lives.

As we returned from a meandering stroll to the top of a hill where hundreds of adult free-range chickens clucked happily in their chicken heaven, we looked out over what she had created at Tara Firma Farms. We took in the green hills, the gardens and the animals. We discussed the problems growers face in going up against modern giant agribusiness, and the difficulty in transforming peoples' consciousness to seek an alternative. At one point Tara turned to me and said something that encapsulated the truth in one succinct sentence: "It's not okay for people to live unconsciously anymore."

When we allow large industries to take over the details of our daily lives, like the food we eat, we give our power away. In chapter five we explored the benefits of taking back some of that power by shopping locally, which keeps dollars in our communities. We can also take our power back by supporting local growers who respect their workers, their animals and the land that gives us sustenance. Find your local farmers' market. Find grocery stores that sell grass-fed, humanely raised meats and locally grown fruits and vegetables. Seek out seasonal foods that can be obtained from closer sources and buy foods that are raised without pesticides or additives. Learn to read the labels on the foods you choose. Take out your lawn and plant a garden.

If every shopper allocated just one or two dollars of their food budget a day toward locally grown foods, we could have thousands of thriving, prosperous farms producing healthy, local foods for everyone. The more knowledge you have the more power you have. When you buy something you are voting with your dollars for the kind of future you want. If you want to be a part of the solution there is plenty of support. Go to the Internet, find a CSA near you and give them a try. Slow Food USA is active and thriving coast to coast and around the world. There is likely a group in your area that would love to welcome you into the fold.

The more people who decide to put their creativity and attention to work on this problem, the more likely we can clean up the toxins and abuse in our food systems and go forward to a healthier, more equitable future. It's up to us as individuals to choose to support life and a healthy food system so we can pass on a healthier, sustainable world.

8

URANIUM, SUNSHINE AND DEAD DINOSAURS: THE SEARCH FOR SUSTAINABLE ENERGY

I believe that the average guy in the street will give up a great deal, if he really understands the cost of not giving it up. In fact, we may find that, while we're drastically cutting our energy consumption, we're actually raising our standard of living.

David R. Brower

What do oil company executives and vampires have in common? They both fear solar energy.

Michio Kaku

Over the past half century issues surrounding energy—how to get it, how to pay for it, how to keep it from destroying the Earth—have created some of the most perplexing problems the globe has ever faced. And the problem *is* global. We are all grappling with it, from the most modern first-world countries to the most impoverished emerging societies, and we will succeed or fail together in finding a solution.

Ever since 1859, when Edwin Drake drilled his first oil well in Northwestern Pennsylvania, America and the rest of the world have become more and more reliant on fossil fuels for those things that keep our societies running. The industrial revolution and all the wonderful inventions that accompanied it have transformed the planet. No longer do we rely on human or animal power; oil, natural gas and coal provide the muscle that drives our economies and our lives. At this point we simply cannot survive with our current lifestyles and comforts without oil. This reliance on fossil fuels has become the most problematic and glaringly visible example of humanity's inability and unwillingness to look down the road and plan for the long term. Quite simply, the problem comes down to this:

*Every*thing our civilization needs to survive into the future—transportation, communications, food, medicine, manufacturing, technology—everything, is dependent on a resource that is finite.

Oil. We can't get to work without it. We can't do our work without it. We can't get through a day without it, and it's running out. It took nature millions of years to create all those hydrocarbon fuels, and it looks like we'll burn through them in just a few hundred years. In the last decade or so the term "peak oil" has been bandied about a lot in the media. It refers to that point in time when we have extracted half of the available oil from the Earth and supplies begin their slow decline.

Though it has only recently come to the attention of the public, the concept of peak oil was first put forth in 1956 by geoscientist Marion King Hubbert in a paper presented to the American Petroleum Institute. Hubbert predicted that America would reach peak oil sometime between the late 1960s and the early 1970s. Some say we have reached peak oil; some say Hubbert's calculations were way off and we have a long way to go before the slippery stuff runs out. Whichever side of the argument you're on, the fact is that if we keep pumping oil out of the ground, sooner or later it will run out. As that happens we'll start fighting over what's left.

Actually we're already fighting wars over oil. The first gulf war, where we went into Kuwait to kick out Iraq's army, was couched as a war to liberate Kuwait; but everyone knew it was about protecting the oil fields in Saudi Arabia. We didn't care about liberating Kuwait. Lots of people protested this, shouting slogans such as "no blood for oil," objecting to killing people to ensure our oil supply.

But the way things are now, access to oil is a gigantic national security issue. There's simply no getting around it. Whether or not we like or approve of it, unless we want the world as we know it to collapse, we must have it. America without oil would be an unpleasant place. A few weeks without it would bring about a complete breakdown of our society—resulting in riots, flames, anarchy, food shortages and lots of other inconveniences. Securing our oil supplies is a legitimate national security issue, but we have painted ourselves into a corner, finding ourselves reliant for our very existence on expensive oil supplies that we are forced to buy from countries that don't like us very much. They're trapped too. They don't like us but they like our money. Without it many oil-producing Middle Eastern countries would have nothing.

Here's something that bothers me a lot about this. Our oil is drilled, pumped and transported by private companies that make profits so large that they eclipse anything seen before in the history of the world. Because we need their product so much, we taxpayers secure those oil supplies for them using the force and might of the American military. Imagine having a company whose product is guarded by the American army, air force and navy. You could just continue raking in the profits while your trade routes, your property, your employees, your entire operation, is protected by the most powerful armed forces in the world. If anyone tries to get in the way of your company's continued operation and profits, brave, young American volunteers will fight to the death far from home to stop them. Even when we're not fighting a war, we keep fleets and armies stationed permanently overseas just in case, and because we like your company so much, we give you billions of dollars in tax credits each year. That would be a pretty sweet deal, but it's exactly what we're doing with oil giants like Exxon and others. Securing our oil supplies is a legitimate national security issue, but if we are going to ask our young people to put their lives on the line for those supplies, the profits should go back to the taxpayers, not a few rich executives.

Gas and oil were cheap for a long time. So cheap that we built our entire society and infrastructure around it. We first got an inkling that we might have a problem back in the 1970s, when the Organization of Petroleum Exporting Countries (OPEC) got mad at us over arms supplies to Israel and created an oil embargo to show their displeasure, creating hours-long lines of gas-guzzling American cars at gas stations across the nation. For the first time America got a good look at how vulnerable we were to the caprices of oil-producing nations. This was a wake-up call, an opportunity to step back and say to ourselves and each other that we need to kick this oil habit or we're going to have a big problem very soon. And we *did* say that. Everyone said it. In fact, every single president since that time has stood up and made a speech about the need to end our "addiction to oil." We moaned and complained, we got angry; we shook our heads and agreed that something really must be done, but in the end, when the OPEC countries decided their point had been made and the oil started flowing again, we got back in our cars and went about our business and the whole mess faded away from the headlines and our consciousness. But the gas prices were higher, and they have climbed steadily higher ever since. Through it all, American car manufacturers continued to crank out large, inefficient cars, and we continued buying them. The problem hadn't gone away, we were just ignoring it. In the short term it was easier to stick our heads in the sand.

In his book, *Collapse: How Societies Choose to Fail or Succeed,* Jared Diamond points out that when a country stakes its future on another country, even a friendly one, its future is dependent on the other country's stability and cooperation. In this case we have staked our future on countries that are not friendly, and often on the edge of political and regional chaos.

Sometimes I imagine it this way: It's like we're on a train traveling at breakneck speed. Up ahead, the track is out. *We all know the track is out* as we race at full throttle toward catastrophe at the end of the line, which gets closer and closer with each passing day. What do we do? We put a brick on the accelerator and pop the champagne and try not to think about it. It's become one of those niggling back-of-the-mind things, like the fact that you still haven't cleaned out the garage like you promised. We're aware of it, but the problem is larger than any one of us can tackle, so we push it to the back burners of our minds.

Since the turn of the 21st century, awareness of this issue has been creeping back into the American consciousness. Car manufacturers continue to build ridiculous, giant vehicles that get lousy mileage, but they are also starting to produce hybrids and smaller, more gas-efficient models. It's a change that's been slow to come, and it isn't nearly enough, but it's welcome nonetheless.

Companies are falling all over each other to tout their greenness. Even oil companies, in an attempt to make us not hate them so much, air ads about the need for alternative energy. And that's a good sign, because when corporations start to talk about something, it's because they know that the public is thinking about it. They want to get on board or at least make us think they have gotten on board, but often corporations aren't really embracing the issue. They spend more money trying to convince us they're environmentally friendly than they spend to actually become environmentally friendly. Corporations, wanting to keep or lure customers, often pretend they are environmentally friendly while continuing business as usual. When they market themselves as greener than they actually are, it's called greenwashing. It's like dusting the Bible because the Pastor is coming to dinner.

Oil companies show commercials depicting children running through fields of flowers and talk about how much they care for the Earth. Cadillac recently came out with a giant "hybrid" SUV, which gets a lousy 21 miles per gallon. They ignore the lousy fuel economy and keep using the word hybrid as though it makes it all okay. Perhaps you've noticed that some car companies have begun stating their mileage in terms of "annual cost of fuel" instead of miles per gallon in an attempt to divert your attention away from the fact that they still get horrible mileage and haven't done a thing to change it. When they tell us they're green while continuing to waste resources and harm the planet, it's like they're pissing on our boot and telling us it's raining.

The Iraq war and other unrest in the Middle East have caused spikes in oil prices that have gotten our attention. Everyone who purchased a Hummer or some giant truck learned how much money it would take to fill the tank. But we can't seem to actually get our heads around the fact that easy access to oil is going to end. We talk about fuel-efficient cars and needing to find alternatives, but we aren't acting in a way that says we're serious.

Change will not come from our leaders; it will come from individuals like you and me who have decided that we are going to make those changes in our own lives. Since we know oil is going to run out, even if lasts a hundred years, wouldn't it seem wiser to begin now the process of transforming our society to reflect that fact? Everyone would agree that figuring it out sooner rather than later would be a good thing, but our economy is so wrapped up in the dominant paradigm that any movement is nearly impossible. We cling to our jobs, industries and fears, and with each passing day the reckoning grows closer.

"King Coal" is the other bogeyman in this scenario. The good news is we still have plenty of it buried right here in America, so much that we have been called "the Saudi Arabia of coal." The bad news is that burning coal causes a lot of damage from pollution. In the U.S. we have hundreds of coal-fired power plants spewing CO_2 into the air. Many are outdated and inefficient. A fossil fuel like oil, coal has long been the main fuel used in power plants across the nation to generate electricity, but burning coal releases arsenic, lead, mercury, dioxins, formaldehyde, benzene and lots of other toxins into the air we breathe. While we have diminished levels of pollution from these plants they are still some of the worst environmental troublemakers.

Their pollutants cause shorter life spans, respiratory illnesses and other health problems. The government's Clean Air Task Force attributes 24,000 deaths annually to coal emissions. In addition, these emissions discolor buildings, damage crops, forests, and soil, pollute our waterways, and degrade ecosystems. According to a report by Environment America titled *America's Biggest Polluters*, in 2007 America's coal burning power plants released 2.56 billion tons of CO_2, the equivalent of that released by 449 million cars. Despite the damage coal-fired plants cause, we're stuck with them for now. They generate about half of the electricity we need to keep the country functioning.

The coal industry and politicians talk about our huge coal reserves and how we can move into the future using "clean coal" technology, but there is no such thing as clean coal. The term refers to methods to eliminate or sequester carbon emissions from burning coal. Though it sounds great, it's a myth. The next time you hear an industry spokesperson or a politician tout the benefits of clean coal, remember: the number of clean coal plants in the world today add up to zero. No effective method to sequester the emissions has yet been found. Coal is touted by the coal industry as a cheap, plentiful fuel, but it's only cheap when you ignore the costs to health and the environment.

We have large coal reserves in America, but the methods used to extract them are creating ecological disasters and costs that are foisted off on society. Robert F. Kennedy Jr., son of the late Senator, is an outspoken critic of the coal industry and the toll it takes on our environment and the people in coal country.

He began a campaign to heighten peoples' awareness of one of the most insidious practices of the coal industry: mountaintop removal. In Appalachia and other areas, the coal companies use high explosives to literally blow the tops off mountains to get to the coal seams that lay underneath.

After the mountaintop is blown to smithereens, gargantuan machines shovel the rubble into adjoining valleys, choking waterways and destroying habitats. According to Kennedy, the Environmental Protection Agency reports that over 1200 miles of rivers and streams have been completely interred by this practice. At least "470 of Appalachia's mountains have simply disappeared." Each week coal companies set off explosives equal to the bomb dropped on Hiroshima, Japan, leveling mountains, destroying forests and leaving behind barren, ravaged moonscapes as large as Manhattan.

Natural gas is cleaner than coal, but needs extensive processing to be usable and still releases a significant amount of CO_2 when burned. While the natural gas industry has been touting natural gas as the bridge fuel that will carry us through the hard times until we come up with alternatives, natural gas comes with its own set of environmental and supply problems. The assumptions about natural gas according to a report titled, "*Will Natural Gas Fuel America in the 21st Century?*" commissioned by the Post-Carbon Institute, are threefold: First, that we have enough natural gas resources in the United States to last 100 years; second, that the price of natural gas will remain low; and third, that natural gas is cleaner and safer than other fossil fuels from the standpoint of greenhouse emissions and public health. The report debunks all three of these assumptions. You can download it for free at http://www.postcarbon.org. The newest method for extracting natural gas is called high-volume horizontal fracturing, or hydrofracking. This method consists of injecting water, sand and chemicals deep into wells under intense hydraulic pressure to fracture the rock and release gas. This produces millions of gallons of wastewater contaminated with carcinogens like benzene, radioactive elements like radium, and corrosive salts, all of which occur naturally deep in the Earth. Coupled with the chemicals used in the fracking process itself, these things find their way into our aquifers and waterways.

Biofuels produced from corn or sugar have received a lot of attention. President George W. Bush signed an energy bill mandating that 36 billion gallons of biofuel per year be used by 2020. When burned, biofuels release less CO_2 than fossil fuels and while growing—like all plants—they absorb CO_2 so they are ostensibly carbon neutral. But it turns out that biofuels come with a higher price than anticipated.

In a study by Princeton University and the Nature Conservancy it was shown that clearing untouched land to grow plants for biofuel releases long-sequestered carbon into the atmosphere. While using already farmed land was fine, the study found that "converting rainforests, peat lands, savannas or grasslands to produce biofuel creates a biofuel carbon debt by releasing 17 to 420 times more carbon dioxide than the fossil fuels they replace." Also, growing plants for fuel precludes growing plants for food. In a world already struggling to feed its growing population, increased dependence on biofuels and the land required to grow them would mean that food shortages could increase.

In the end, even if the oil, coal, gas and biofuels would last for a million years, they all emit CO_2 when burned, and supplies aside, it's the CO_2 that is turning out to be the biggest problem of all.

In the fifties, a young scientist named Charles David Keeling from Scranton, Pennsylvania, began an experiment to answer a question floating through scientific circles. Was the CO_2 being produced by burning fossil fuels ending up in the atmosphere, or was it being absorbed by the oceans and plants of the world? From the summit of Mauna Loa volcano on the island of Hawaii, Keeling took air samples at regular intervals and over time discovered that CO_2 levels were rising. The amount of CO_2 in the atmosphere fluctuated seasonally as plants bloomed or died off to absorb more or less of it, but the mean amount was rising steadily, measured by what came to be called the Keeling Curve.

In 1958, when he began his measurements, the CO_2 levels were 315 parts per million (ppm). By 2005, that number reached 380 ppm. Keeling and other scientists realized that if CO_2 levels continued to rise, they could potentially affect the Earth's temperature. The CO_2 would act as a "greenhouse," trapping the Earth's heat within the atmosphere, causing global warming.

Global warming—climate change—has become a huge political and environmental issue for the world. On one hand leaders are trying to address an outcry from environmental groups. On the other hand, they are shackled by business interests and a stagnant economy. Business interests usually win these debates. The argument over whether human-induced climate change is even happening has begun to wane. Nearly all countries and well over 95 percent of scientists are convinced that it is, but some claim that global warming is a myth even though the science behind the theory is sound. The average temperature of our planet has risen one degree over the last century. This doesn't sound like much until you consider that the difference between our world's average temperature now and the average temperature during the last ice age was only around nine degrees. When it comes to climate, a little goes a long way.

We have already increased the amount of greenhouse gasses in our atmosphere by over 30 percent, and show no signs of stopping. If we raise the temperature by only several degrees over the next century we will experience apocalyptic consequences—from melting polar ice caps leading to rising sea levels and destroyed coastal cities, to extreme storms, droughts, plant and animal extinctions and threats to our food supplies. It's not a pretty picture. We are already experiencing the first stages of this.

Vice President Dick Cheney once said, in speaking about the threat of nuclear terrorism, that if there were a one-percent chance of it happening we must treat it as a certainty in our response, a comment that came to be known as The One-Percent Doctrine. When it comes to humans causing global warming—which could bring global consequences far worse than a single nuclear terrorism incident—the percentages are way above one percent. If 95 percent of scientists agreed about anything else, as they agree about global warming, we would all take notice.

Part of the problem with greenhouse gasses is that we can't see or smell them. We have to take someone's word that they even exist. If all the CO_2 we have released into the air were visible, if it were turning the skies yellow, if we all woke up to a terrible stench every day, if it stained our carpets, we would leap to do something about it. But we can't see or smell it, so it's difficult to realize what is happening. We aren't motivated enough yet to change things, but *if we knew* that by not changing our energy policies we would all die horribly in 10 years, we would have the motivation to solve the problem, even if it meant the disruption of our comfortable lives. I believe that we are approaching a tipping point in our collective consciousness and that soon something big will happen that will scare us and galvanize us to action. It will be a moment when reality slaps us across the face and yells, "Snap out of it!"

The federal government has put some regulations in effect that limit the amounts of greenhouse gasses released by industry and there are rules about maximum emissions from cars. All of these changes were hard won, resisted tooth and nail by the energy and automotive industries. But even as we attempt to rein in our own emissions, countries like China and India that have watched enviously over the years as America prospered are now getting into the game, ramping up construction, building factories and importing or building automobiles at a great rate. Today China burns more coal than the United States, Japan and Europe combined.

At a recent international climate change conference there was great debate over who should foot the bill for proposed changes needed to lower CO_2 levels. America wanted the emerging countries to do their part. The emerging countries said in effect, hey, you've had *your* fun; you're the one who caused this in the first place. If you want change then you pay for it or get out of our way. It's our turn to live the good life. You can't really blame them. But we are all missing the point. Lowering greenhouse emissions is good, but in the long run the entire planet needs to find a viable alternative to oil. We need to reduce dependence on oil, coal, and gas. Our system of endless growth fueled by cheap hydrocarbon energy cannot continue forever.

Canadian scientist David Hughes is passionate and bluntly realistic about this problem. After 30 years with the Geological Survey of Canada, he has come to the conclusion that we are—right now—bumping up against the limits of nature's ability to sustain our industrial societies. He and others believe that most estimates of the energy still available to power industrial society are wildly optimistic. His message is that we've already burned most of the easily captured fuels—the low-hanging fruit. What's left will be continuously more difficult and expensive to get at, and most of it will never be produced because the act of extracting it uses more oil than it yields.

"Unfortunately," said Hughes, "we've overshot the ecological ability of the planet to sustain us, so we're looking at a descent paradigm. We have to look at what will likely be decades of managed descent to get down to some level that's more sustainable. And I think we can do that in two ways: We can keep shoveling bailout money trying to resurrect the growth paradigm that we've been so comfortable with, and hit the wall, and then let Mother Nature take over—and Mother Nature has a way of fixing resource depletion issues; she's done it many times in the past and she'll do it again—or, we can basically realize where we're at now, and where we have to go and start intelligently managing the descent."

Managing the descent sounds grim, but it doesn't have to be. It's a matter of waking up and realizing that what we are doing will not work for much longer. If we all worked together it could be an exciting, positive change. As David Hughes pointed out, if we don't do it, Mother Nature will do it for us, but we must start now. There is no time left squabble over money, power, or support for the way we've been doing things.

We've already seen what happens when we stretch further in our attempts to get at the more difficult-to-extract oil. The Deepwater Horizon oil spill in the Gulf of Mexico in 2010 underscores what can, and will, continue happening in our quest to keep the oil flowing. Many Americans think the answer to "getting off Arab oil" is to aggressively go after existing oil deposits in our own country, many of which are currently off limits because of environmental laws. They cry "drill, baby, drill," ignoring the fact that even if we tapped everything we could, it would barely reduce our dependence on foreign oil, and potentially create more incidents like the Gulf spill.

The Deepwater Horizon debacle arose from corporate interests putting profit over safety, and forcing everyone else to bear the brunt of the damage even as they continued to reap profits. Once again, a company put something dangerous in motion for which they had no plan B. There is no reason to think that if we continue dangerous deep water drilling or drilling in delicate ecological preserves that this will not happen again.

Even if we decide to continue our current paradigm of going forward as if the oil will last forever, the supplies will become harder to access and the price will continue to rise. The price of oil has risen sharply recently due to unrest in the Middle East and Wall Street speculation. When that happened and the price of a gallon of gasoline inched over four dollars, it became front-page news, immediately affecting every sector of the economy. People couldn't buy other things because they were spending all their cash on gas. They couldn't afford to buy the gas to get to work. Some demanded that the government open the Strategic Petroleum Reserve, a stockpile of oil and gasoline kept for emergencies, but opening the Reserve would not affect the price of gas and the entire reserve would only last for about a month at current levels of oil consumption.

Deepwater drilling or opening the oil reserves in not an answer. The answer is to put our heads together and figure out a future that doesn't depend on cheap, easy-to-access oil, and to drastically reduce our energy consumption. But what do we do in the meantime? If we don't want to burn coal and oil, what can we use to replace these things? The other choices are hydroelectric, solar, wind and nuclear.

We had a couple of bad experiences a while back with nuclear energy. The meltdowns at Three-Mile Island in the United States and Chernobyl in the Soviet Union made many decide that the benefits of nuclear power weren't worth the risks, but the nuclear power industry didn't go away. Over time many more plants were built around the globe.

The thing about nuclear power is that it's really great until it's not. It's clean and quiet and hums along, cranking out those megawatts nicely until something horrible happens, and when it does it can render entire regions uninhabitable for hundreds of years and kill lots of people. Nuclear power proponents will point out that the number of people killed by nuclear power plants is tiny compared to other forms of energy, which is true. The disaster at Three-Mile Island killed nobody directly. At Chernobyl 31 people were killed as a direct result of the explosion, but there was an unquantifiable number of cancer deaths from the fallout. The numbers range from 4,000 to over 900,000, depending on the source.

In his book, *Whole Earth Discipline: An Ecopragmatist's Manifesto*, environmentalist Stewart Brand came out in favor of nuclear power, pointing out that it's the best of a lot of bad choices, and the newer, more modern nuclear plants were smaller and much safer. He also pointed out that the nuclear industry is aware of the public's distrust, and know that one bad accident can destroy their industry, so they won't allow this to happen.

Then in spring of 2011, a huge earthquake hit the northern coast of Japan, followed by a tsunami that swept in and engulfed the Fukushima nuclear power plant, causing three reactors to meltdown. The resulting fallout could be measured in the Pacific Northwest of the United States. Thousands of Japanese were forced to evacuate the contaminated area, perhaps forever. After Fukushima, Germany passed legislation to shut down their entire nuclear power industry, all 17 reactors, by 2022. In Japan they will be dealing with this disaster for generations to come.

Beyond accidents, the other quandary with nuclear power is that while it solves an energy problem in the short run, it creates one of the longest-term conundrums we've ever faced, waste that will remain dangerous to human life for a period of time longer than our recorded history. We have trouble thinking into next week. Something that will have to be dealt with for thousands of years is effectively beyond our scope.

One of the biggest problems the Japanese had to deal with after the tsunami hit the Fukushima nuclear plant was the spent nuclear rods stored in outdoor pools that had became unstable from the quake and flood. Storing nuclear waste this way is common. Until we come up with something better, many places around the United States and the world put highly radioactive spent fuel in "temporary" holding tanks, submerging them in water for years to cool them. Many nuclear plants in America are running out of space in their storage pools. In the meantime, the rods sit there waiting for a permanent home or to kill someone, whichever comes first. There are dry cask storage methods as well, but neither these nor storage pools are considered permanent.

The U.S. government did find a spot that was thought to be a good place to dispose of nuclear waste. Yucca Mountain in Nevada is dry, stable and considered safe for long-term storage of spent fuel from our nuclear plants. Our government spent billions preparing this site to receive this waste. And this brings up a story of one rare example of our government actually trying to think deeply long term.

Author and astrophysicist Gregory Benford, in his book *Deep Time: How Humanity Communicates Across Millennia,* described a phone call he received asking him to participate on a panel of scientists, sociologists and other forward thinkers. It seems that as congress was thinking about Yucca Mountain as a possible place to store spent nuclear rods, they had actually considered the future. How, they wondered, could we communicate to future generations for at least ten thousand years that they should stay away from the spent nuclear waste? They couldn't assume that anyone would speak English thousands of years in the future, or know how to read. They couldn't assume there would be a United States. They couldn't assume anything. So they commissioned a panel of experts to solve the problem of making sure that anyone who happened across this dangerous place in the future would get the crystal-clear message that it's very dangerous and they should not go in.

The panel failed to come up with something they knew would work because it's not possible to know or understand what cultures, beliefs or motivations humans will have that far in the future. I only brought it up because I was impressed that it had occurred to our representatives to even ask the question.

But the question underscores the problem. There is no good way to deal with nuclear waste. We can't shoot it into space because there is too much chance of a rocket blowing up and spreading it all over the place. We can't just throw it in the ocean. We can't put it in your backyard. So we keep putting it in temporary holding pools and pass the problem on to the future. Yucca Mountain, by the way, was never approved and funded for nuclear waste storage, though we spent billions preparing it. As of this writing, we still don't have any long-term plan to dispose of nuclear waste.

Solar and wind power hold great promise, though neither has an effective way to store energy. But the sun and wind are free, clean energy sources and it would be worth the time and expense to figure out how to take advantage of them. It has been calculated that about 100 square miles of modern solar panels would generate enough energy to power the United State's entire energy grid. Several states have the room and the sunshine. A March 2007 study for the Department of Energy found that Arizona, New Mexico, California, Utah, Colorado and Texas are the top states, in that order, to generate solar power. Together they have the resources and land to generate more than 16,000 terawatt hours per year from solar energy. Total U.S. electricity generation in 2007 was about 4000 terawatt hours. In California, solar panel systems covering a 30-by-30 square mile area could produce 300 terawatt hours, enough to supply the entire state. Eleven percent of New Mexico's land could be used to power the entire U.S. grid.

Instead of concentrating all the power generation into one place, as we do now with large power plants, we could spread it out over a large area of smaller power generators, each connected to the whole. If each state built five square miles of solar panels connected on one giant grid, we'd have more power than we could use. Some areas would have more sunlight and create more power, but all would be a part of a large, sustainable grid, each sending power where it's needed. We already have millions of existing buildings with a massive amount of roof space. We could outfit them all with solar panels, each using what they need and pumping the rest back into the grid.

I have often wondered why it's not a law that all new buildings that use electricity be required to have solar panels. If we converted our national power grid to a system with thousands of power-generating buildings or small areas dedicated to solar panels or wind generators, our grid would be invulnerable to terrorism. Any damage would only hurt a small part of the whole. It would decentralize the system, take the power out of the hands of oil companies, and make each region of the country more sustainable and independent. Instead of one power plant failing and plunging us into darkness, we could all connect together and send all the power we need to wherever it's needed.

Centralizing large systems, whether they are mega food producers, retailers with giant central distribution centers, or power companies where one plant serves millions of customers, limits choices and make the whole system, and all of us, more vulnerable. This idea of decentralization is worth exploring.

In his fascinating book, *Out of Control: The New Biology of Machines, Social Systems, and the Economic World*, author Kevin Kelly described a group of scientists grappling with the science of robotics, specifically in regard to sending them to explore other planets in our solar system. After many attempts and experiments the scientists realized that the classic model of a robot, with its entire computer power centrally located and controlling every aspect of the robot, was flawed. They were trying to develop adaptable robots that could learn as they went about their business millions of miles from home with minimum supervision.

The team discovered that when they concentrated all the power in one place, the robots had trouble solving unexpected problems and handling too many inputs from too many sources. To solve this, they tried decentralizing the brainpower of the robots. Instead of one central brain, they designed them so that each different part of the robot had its own processor, specifically designed to do its one task only when needed and report its findings to the other brains. One massive processor didn't have to know and try to control everything at once. The robots designed this way were much more nimble in solving tasks and had fewer breakdowns. If one processor broke down, the others still worked and the mission could go forward.

For much of the 20th century the world struggled between two models of government, communism and capitalism. The Soviet Union had a model that concentrated all of its power and decision-making tasks in the government. The government told the washing machine factories what kinds of washing machines to make and how many. They told the farmers what to grow and they told the stores what they could sell, how much and for what price. Every decision in their society came from the top down. It didn't matter if nobody wanted that kind of washing machine, or if there was anybody to buy them. The government controlled everything. This led to a stagnant and cumbersome economy that never became successful. The Soviet Union may have been a "superpower," but only militarily. The rest of their economy never managed to function well.

In America individual citizens and towns were allowed to decide what they wanted to manufacture, grow or sell. If there was a market for their product, they succeeded. If not, they could do something else. We ended up with millions of businesses owned by millions of people, serving millions of others. This incredible variety of minds and ideas is what allowed America to be so nimble when it came to innovation and creativity. This system came with its own downside, as capitalism can be predatory and take unfair advantage of others. By creating a system that did not have power concentrated in one entity, America leaped ahead of the world in many areas. Ironically, many of the problems we are now facing stem from businesses growing so large that power has become more and more concentrated in a few corporations.

Consider the Internet. It is a stupendously huge creation with billions of Web sites put up by untold numbers of humans, yet it has no location. There's no building with a big sign on the front that says "The Internet." It grew organically, and exists in billions of computers around the globe. Like Kevin Kelly's robots, each piece contributes to the whole only when and where it's needed.

A power grid could act the same way, with thousands of locations contributing to the whole. It would be expensive and a huge, difficult project. New infrastructure would be needed. Thousands of miles of wiring and electrical systems would have to be installed. It has been estimated that the cost would approach six trillion dollars. With oil at just 100 dollars a barrel—and it's often higher—we could spend six trillion dollars on oil in less than eight years.

But the cost we really need to consider is the cost of doing nothing. For if we do nothing we are surely headed toward a future of pain and catastrophe. We need to ask these questions and ponder these possibilities now, but those who own the oil or coal companies, and those whose livelihoods are tied to them, will fight tooth and nail to prevent anything from changing the current model. After all, millions of people are directly or indirectly employed by and dependent on these industries.

To change things is not only to come up with a different vision for our future; it's to change the foundational worldview and way of life for those millions and everyone else. When something threatens jobs people become afraid and politicians pander to this fear. Politicians of both parties from coal states fight for the coal industries and the jobs they bring, even when they know it's ruining the environment. To do otherwise would get them voted out of office quickly. The hard fact we need to face is that the changes we need to bring about will be difficult. People don't like change. In America we don't like to sacrifice anything. We talk about sacrificing, for freedom, for rights, for the American way of life, but we don't like to actually do it. We have embraced the attitude that anything that feels bad, is hard or asks us to revisit our basic assumptions about what we're entitled to is completely unacceptable. Vice President Dick Cheney summed this up when he said, "The American way of life is non-negotiable."

Confronted with something that isn't working, we in the West tend to look outside of ourselves for the fix. We want to treat the symptoms, not the root cause of problems. Gas is too expensive? Don't try to figure out a lifestyle that is less dependent on it, instead get mad at the government or gas companies and demand they make it affordable again so you never have to change anything about how you live your life.

Assuming that the answers to our problems are someone else's responsibility makes us victims. Looking outside of ourselves for answers while ignoring the fact that we have shared responsibility for the problems we're facing keeps us from realizing our own power and freedom. The problems with fossil fuels are no exception. Each of us is part of the problem. If we could step back and look at it with a long-term viewpoint, we would realize that each of us could do much to alleviate the problem. Changing our oil economy may take a while, but we can do so much now, without waiting for our leaders, by reducing our use of fossil fuels.

Little things can go a long way if enough people do them. Sometimes the answer to a problem becomes apparent if we step outside our normal thinking patterns.

I once read a story about a Central American country that was facing an energy problem for its growing population. They had decided to build a large hydroelectric dam on a major river running through this country. The dam would, like all dams, alter the ecology of the country and create many problems with their ecosystems that would need to be addressed in the future, and it would be very expensive. As the dam was being planned and argued over, a group of long-term thinkers did a side study that delved deeper into the country's energy problems. Nearly all the households in the country were using old, inefficient appliances from the fifties. They concluded that if every household in the country was simply given a brand new, energy-efficient refrigerator, enough energy would be saved to eliminate the need for the dam, at a cost hundreds of times lower, but the momentum behind building the dam was too great. Like using energy-efficient refrigerators to reduce power demand, there are things we can do collectively in our own country that could make a profound impact on our energy woes.

Nobel prize-winning scientist Steven Chu, appointed by President Obama to the position of Secretary of Energy, offered up this simple, elegant idea. He figured out that if all of us painted our roofs white to reflect heat, we would reduce global carbon emissions by an amount equal to taking all the world's cars off the road for 11 years. A few cans of whitewash each would be a small price to pay for such a benefit. The new compact fluorescent light bulbs that have come onto the market recently are more energy efficient than traditional incandescent bulbs, which turn much of the energy they consume into heat instead of light. The federal Energy Star program notes that if each U.S. household replaced just five old incandescent bulbs with new compact fluorescent bulbs, we could shut down 24 power plants.

Right now, somewhere in your house there is a VCR, or a coffee pot or a phone charger, with a little light-emitting diode (LED). Maybe it's showing the time, maybe it's an indicator showing that it's plugged in; but if it's lit, it's drawing power. The cost of keeping those little lights on is very small on our individual power bills, to the point were it doesn't warrant our attention, but collectively—nationally—there are hundreds of millions of LEDs sucking energy off the grid, and not doing much else. It adds up.

An article in the *New York Times* pointed out that the so-called set-top boxes, those boxes we use to bring cable television into our homes, have become the single largest electricity drain in our homes. Because of the time these devices need to boot up after being turned off the manufacturers designed then to exist in an always-on configuration, citing that customers would complain if they had to wait a few minutes to watch TV. There are 160 million of these set-top boxes in the U.S., one for every two people. The article pointed out that, "many homes now have one or more basic cable boxes as well as add-on digital video recorders, which use 40 percent more power than the set-top box. A study by the Natural Resources Defense Council concluded that the boxes consumed $3 billion in electricity per year in the United States, and that 66-percent of that power is being wasted when no one is watching and shows are not being recorded."

Office buildings often have their lights on all day, even if a room isn't being used. At home we leave computers on, or leave the monitors on when we turn off the computer. When you add up all this power usage it is a huge drain on our resources, and a simple thing to fix. Turn off the light. Unplug the coffee pot. Design cable boxes that don't consume energy when they're not being used. Buy a car that gets good mileage.

I don't want to sound like a grumpy, dour uncle telling you to quit complaining, turn down the heat and put on a sweater, but there are many things we can do that would help create a more secure nation energy-wise, and buy us time as we figure out how to transition away from a carbon economy. I have talked several times in this book about the power of the collective. When enough people decide to change what they're doing and embark on wiser, healthier course, a movement can take on a life of its own and have an amazing impact on the world. We are already using the power of the collective when it comes to energy, but we are collectively doing the wrong things. Our energy consumption stays high, our cars stay large and we continue to try and figure out how to go forward without making any changes, and without taking a hard look at what we can do to be part of the solution instead of part of the problem.

Our future doesn't have to be a scary, apocalyptic nightmare. If enough of us choose this, it can be a future of reality-based decisions that take the long-term health of the globe into consideration, not just our country, our state, our city or our house. When we widen our scope of thinking to embrace the long view, to embrace the whole, it will embrace us back.

9

NATURE CAN STILL TEACH US A THING OR TWO

Never does nature say one thing
and wisdom another.

Juvenal

We have come a long way in our exploration of long-term thinking and investigated many problems inherent with short sightedness and its effects on our lives and our world. We have explored deep time and seen how our frantic pace of life affects our happiness, pondered our loss of community and investigated the challenges we face with debt, community, consumerism, agriculture and energy, all with an eye toward the long term. While our problems may seem insurmountable, tied as they are to a system so large and intractable, there is a lot we can do to nudge things in the right direction. Fortunately, when we find ourselves wondering what the right course of action may be, we have a wonderful teacher we can turn to for answers, that wise old gal Mother Nature herself.

To tap the wisdom of nature, we have to realize that we are, in fact, part of nature. This is something we forget as we cloak ourselves in the trappings of intellect and technology. Humans, with our self-awareness and ability to use tools and alter our environment, slip easily into the fiction that we are somehow apart from or above nature. We often feel that if nature gets in our way, we can alter things to suit us, ignoring the natural forces that still play out behind our schemes. We behave like newly arrived colonists on someone else's beach, as though nature is something to be subjugated and conquered. Just plant the flag in the ground and start tearing things up.

We do this at our peril. Mother Nature can be covered up, pushed around, or ignored for a while, but she always wins in the long run. When she enforces her laws, she does it dispassionately and without favoritism. In nature, as in our own penal system, ignorance of the law is no excuse. Conversely, every step we take toward living in balance and harmony with nature is a step toward a better future, a better past and a better now. Nature always takes the long view and we have much to learn from her if we can get out of our own short-term way and pay attention. To create true sustainability and long-term happiness we need to work with nature, not against her.

Biomimicry studies nature's best ideas and then tries to imitate them and apply them to our own endeavors. For example, scientists are trying to understand how a spider can weave a web that is stronger than steel, or how a mollusk can create a hard, ceramic-like shell, both using no heat and only the materials at hand—not changing nature, but imitating her. Unlocking secrets like these could solve many problems and spring technology forward to a more sustainable future. There are simpler, easier-to-understand lessons to be learned from nature, hidden in plain sight, and often ignored.

Let's look at nine things that can be learned from nature's example and that we can apply to our personal lives and society. Some of these things may overlap a bit but each is important to consider on its own in order to get a holistic picture of the problem. A pilot guiding a jumbo liner through the skies has lots of different things to pay attention to—flaps, speed, fuel, engine oil, navigation—and knows that forgetting any of them serves up the same consequence. Likewise, each separate lesson from nature is equally important.

1. Unending Growth is Impossible

The tide goes in, the tide goes out; the moon waxes and wanes and the seasons change, each in their turn. Species come and go; mountains rise and fall; islands appear and disappear and ice creeps down to cover the continents, then creeps back, only to come again.

Our planet and our universe work in cycles. In circles. Our individual lives are comprised of many circles, from small to large, each coming back to the starting point. We inhale; we exhale. We sleep; we awaken. We are born; we die. Everything nature puts forth, she pulls back, only to put it forth again as the circle comes around. Every period of growth is followed by a period of dormancy. Every period of rest is followed by renewal, and the circle goes around again.

The cyclical nature of the universe is not a secret. We live it every day and see it everywhere we turn; it is woven into the very fabric of our existence. Yet we have created a system of economics predicated on unending growth, blithely ignoring the fact that it is not possible. We expect the value of our homes to rise forever. We expect our salaries to go up every year. We expect our businesses to expand and the nation's economy to grow without end.

By creating a system that sees anything but growth as a failure, we have in effect doomed ourselves to the very failure we fear. Using higher profits as the only yardstick with which to measure success, we miss out on opportunities to celebrate success in other ways. We could, if we chose, celebrate the success of a business by its ability to find a sustainable niche that benefits the customers, the employees and the planet, but we are taught to be dissatisfied with a level playing field, that the only acceptable goal is ever higher profits. Many of us have worked at jobs where the team is given a profit goal, or a sales quota for the quarter or the year. These goals are motivational, and help focus the efforts of the company, but over time they are self defeating. As anyone who has successfully achieved a company goal knows that, when we achieve them, we are rewarded with higher goals. Forever.

With today's economic problems, some people say that the current generation of young people will be the first in U.S. history who won't do "better" than their parents, but we're only measuring that by whether the kids of today will have more money and stuff than their parents. Maybe there's an upside to this. Maybe the next generation will be the first in our history to understand that the endless pursuit of money and possessions is a goal not worth pursuing and fated to fail, *that endless growth is not possible*. Maybe this new generation will be the first to understand that there is more than one way to measure success and happiness.

Vice President Al Gore said in his book *Earth in the Balance*, "Better profits are important; equally important is a frequent side effect to reconcile profitability with a larger social good. Companies that pursue this fresh approach often see a new sense of common purpose arise, a feeling among employees and managers alike that their work has new dignity and their lives have new meaning, because they are not only earning profits and paychecks but are also joining the pursuit of a greater goal."

If we expect our incomes, lifestyles and economies to grow forever, we will be disappointed because it's not going to happen. Instead, we can structure our lives and our economy to pursue goals and expectations that are possible, with built-in expectations of dormancy and renewal. Raj Patel said, "What needs to be plucked out of markets is the perpetual and overriding hunger for expansion and profit that has brought us to the brink of ecological catastrophe; what needs to be plucked out of *us* is the belief that markets are the only way to value our world."

When we learn this we will learn that true happiness and satisfaction does not come from chasing false promises, but from living in accordance with reality. The wider we cast our attention, the larger the natural cycles we can bring into our everyday awareness and the more we will feel compelled to act responsibly. The circles always come back.

2. Waste Nothing

When you walk through a meadow, a forest or an open field, you will step over twigs, dead leaves, insects and the occasional dead bird or rodent. This detritus has not been thrown out by nature; it isn't waste. It is all being absorbed back into the system. Everything in nature is recycled to nurture and support the next generation of plants and animals living there.

Nature wastes nothing. Mountains become rocks that become gravel that is turned into soil. Trees and plants become mulch that nourishes that soil and the life that exists there. Dead animals are eaten by insects; they decompose in the ground, paying the Earth back with nutrients that were borrowed for a short time. This system of recycling is why healthy ecosystems can exist for so long. They do not deplete their resources; they recycle them in a different form.

We, on the other hand, waste a lot. For example, our modern, consumer-driven economy demands that we package the products we sell so we can ship them, display them and protect them. I bought a razor packaged in a nearly impenetrable plastic blister pack. When I finally was able to open it and extract the razor, I was stunned at the amount of waste I was left with. Cardboard, plastic, metal twist ties covered with plastic, booklets with warranty information, the pile of trash dwarfed the actual product. Packaging like this is common. According to Time Magazine, Americans throw away 1.4 billion pounds of waste every day, and 40 percent of it comes from one-time packaging.

Each week garbage services across the country pick up the trash we leave by the curb and cart it off to landfills. Some of these landfills are staggeringly huge, and continue to grow with no end in sight. All of that trash paper, plastic, wood, metal and food combined represents the waste of an enormous amount of energy that was needed to harvest, manufacture and transport those items. This energy is ultimately lost in landfills.

When we extract resources from the ground to manufacture packaging, which is thrown away, we squander something that cannot be replaced. It is not something we can continue to do for the long term. The spoof newspaper *The Onion*, once ran a headline that read: "How Bad for the Environment Can Throwing Away One Plastic Bottle Be 30 Million People Wonder." One plastic bottle may seem like no big deal, but multiply that by millions and it has a huge impact. Here again is the power of the collective; there are a lot of us, and the things we do add up quickly.

We have made great strides in recycling. Walmart actually changed the packaging requirements for their suppliers in an effort to cut waste. But there is much more to be done. We could bring our own bags to the supermarket or say no when we buy something small and are asked if we want a bag—which we will throw away the moment we get home. This is just a matter of breaking a habit. Merchants are in the habit of offering bags; consumers are in the habit of accepting them, even if the bag isn't needed.

Some towns have put laws into effect banning plastic grocery bags, and some stores give discounts to those who bring their own reusable bags. Buying reusable cloth bags to take to the store is easy and can quickly become a good new habit. Here's an eye-opener: According to PlanetGreen.com, while you read this paragraph, 60 thousand plastic bags were used in this country, an amount used every five seconds.

Think about how many people go each day to Starbucks or some other coffee shop and walk out carrying a paper cup with a cardboard sheath to protect their hands from the heat, topped with a plastic lid, all of which is tossed away within minutes. When they go back, they get another cup of paper/cardboard/ plastic and do it again. Imagine for a moment that you could see every paper coffee cup bought in America in one day all piled in one place. How large do you suppose the pile of plastic and cardboard would be? According to the paper industry, in 2010 Americans used around 23 billion paper cups, *all* of which ended up in landfills. The Housing and Food Services Department at the University of Washington reported that its students throw away 5000 cups every school day. Reusable to-go cups cost more initially in both materials and resources, but studies show that the tipping point for energy savings comes at 24 uses. After that, your reusable cup makes a positive impact on our environment and becomes part of the solution. Plus, most coffee shops give a discount when you bring your own cup. It's that simple.

Now is the time to start deliberately buying products that use less packaging, or use packaging that is recyclable, and letting companies know that you're basing your buying decisions on that. We also need to take advantage of whatever recycling programs our town offers.

If you sail out into the Pacific Ocean you might eventually arrive at a place known as the Great Pacific Garbage Patch, an area where ocean current patterns converge—sweeping whatever was riding those currents to one place: mostly plastic, non-biodegradable trash. A toxic soup of garbage bags, plastic bottles and other debris covers an area larger than Texas. Ships report sailing through this plastic garbage for days. In some places studies have found there are six pounds of plastic for every pound of plankton.

The long-lasting plastics are ingested by wildlife; their toxins are absorbed into the oceanic ecosystems causing widespread problems, including death. As the world has gotten smaller, our impact has grown larger. We can no longer use the oceans, rivers or valleys as garbage dumps. We need to realize that we can't throw anything away, because there is no "away."

The concept of Earth as a spaceship and all of us its crew, was first put forth by Kenneth Boulding in a lecture in 1966. Here is part of what he had to say regarding using the Earth as a dump. "As long as man was small in numbers and limited in technology, he could realistically regard the Earth as an infinite reservoir, an infinite source of inputs and an infinite cesspool for outputs. Today we can no longer make this assumption. Earth has become a space ship, not only in our imagination but also in the hard realities of the social, biological, and physical system in which man is enmeshed. In what we might call the "old days," when man was small in numbers and Earth was large, he could pollute it with impunity, though even then he frequently destroyed his immediate environment and had to move on to a new spot, which he then proceeded to destroy. Now man can no longer do this; he must live in the whole system, in which he must recycle his wastes and really face up to the problem of the increase in material entropy, which his activities create. In a space ship there are no sewers."

It doesn't matter what you do, but do *something*, because collectively even the smallest changes help.

3. Nature Seeks Balance

The overarching design of the universe is one of balance. Its parameters may change from season to season or year to year, but balance is always attained. Nature likes to even things up. If there is more rain one year, there will be more plants, so rabbits will have more babies. When there are more rabbits, birds of prey will lay more eggs. When white-tailed deer see too many other white butts scampering around, they will slow their reproduction rates to keep from overpopulating and straining resources. If too many rabbits, hawks or any other animal (say humans), are born, and there are not enough resources to support them, nature will decrease the population through starvation or some other means until balance is found again. It's harsh, but it's sustainable. It's an exquisite ballet, a balance of resources and a balance of opposing forces.

Our moon orbits the Earth in a balanced dance of gravity and centrifugal force. Ecosystems—whether a pond, a vast grassland, a rain forest, or an icy mountain—support life in a delicate balance of predator and prey, plant and animal, growth and reduction, birth and death. There is always a balance between the populations of great grazing herds and the grasses to support them. There is always a balance between action and dormancy, male and female, light and dark. Plants produce oxygen for the animals; animals produce CO_2 for the plants in an eternal give and take. Even the weather is nature seeking balance. Warmer air, heated by sunshine on the land, rises. As it rises, air rushes in from the sides to fill the space left behind.

It's a never-ending process of nature balancing things out in an ever-changing world.

Nature can be thought of as a Vaudeville act, riding a unicycle while spinning plates on sticks and juggling, all in perfect balance. Change the smallest thing and the rest must either adjust (and the ability to adjust and stay balanced diminishes with each change) or come to a crashing halt. Nature is adaptable and resilient and can absorb much, but we're getting close to kicking the unicycle out from under her.

Nothing can survive for long if it gets too far out of balance with nature. Each organism, and each cell in that organism, has to work with the forces around it or pay the price. We tend to ignore this law of nature, acting like we are foreign officials with diplomatic immunity, flashing our diplomatic plates at the authorities and scoffing at the laws. Right now we're busy unbalancing the ratio of CO_2 in the atmosphere, upsetting a natural balance of carbon sequestration as old as life itself. When we force something out of balance we can get away with it for a period of time and we may think we're winning, but nature operates on a long scale and in the end—no matter how much technology we throw at it—she will find a way to balance things out.

Balance not only applies to large systems. It applies to our individual lives as well. Many of us live our lives out of balance. We eat too much, drink too much, sit too much, worry too much and fear too much. Living under so much stress from money or career woes, we no longer feel in tune with the world around us and we lose sight of the big picture. For many, life has become a never-ending race to the finish line, filled with consternation, fear, guilt, pressure, resentment and sadness.

When we lose sight of what is important in the long run, when we forget that we are a part of something larger than ourselves, it causes pain, disease and suffering. It's time to step back, take a breath and look around at our world, and deep inside ourselves. It's time to take the long view. Seeking balance in all things not only restores and maintains health and happiness; it is essential for a sustainable future.

4. Diversity In Everything Is Necessary and Healthy

Nature likes to mix things up. A diverse ecosystem is resilient and healthy. When you walk in nature you are surrounded by myriad species of animals and plants. Dozens of different types of insects may inhabit the same patch of grass. Different plants, animals, birds, insects and bacteria have evolved to live together in nature. They have developed a way to do this that allows every species to continue. Each of these species has a different job to do, and each contributes to the whole.

This diversity is found in individual species as well. Look at us. We're tall and short, black and white, blue eyed and brown eyed, gay and straight, blond, redheaded and more. This diversity is what keeps us going as a species. The less diversity there is, the greater the chance for a disease or other disaster to damage the species. This is why incest is illegal or taboo in nearly every culture worldwide. The more we mix up the genes, the healthier we are. Dog lovers know that mutts are generally healthier than purebred dogs. Highly inbred dogs are known to have problems—depending on the breed—such as hip dysplasia or short life spans. This comes from over-breeding from a shallow gene pool.

The benefits of diversity don't just apply to ecosystems. A large part of America's success is that it has always been a nation of immigrants. People from all over the world come to the U.S. and bring their unique worldviews and skills to bear on the society, all of which contribute to a more vibrant and forward-thinking society. Regular infusions of new worldviews, new thoughts and new perspectives make for an exciting future of possibilities. Without them, societies can become stagnant, trapped in their narrow beliefs and views while the world moves on without them. Even our local economies are healthier when we have a diverse range of stores and services, rather than one looming corporate presence providing everything.

Our society, agriculture, economy, civilization and species need diversity for health, resilience and long-term viability. Governments that strive to stifle new or conflicting views become isolated from the world and ultimately from their own people. The more ideas, the more viewpoints and the more creative approaches to problems found within a society, the more likely it is that the society will thrive.

I have always been impressed with the tradition of Native American societies when it comes to diversity. Many Native American tribes were happy to bring new people into the fold. When they captured women or children of other races or tribes, they often incorporated the women into their tribes and raised the children as their own. The color of the skin wasn't the important thing; it was their culture. Anyone could be raised to be a Comanche or an Apache.

When Lewis and Clark made their journey of discovery, William Clark took his slave, York, on the trip across the continent. Many of the Native Americans they encountered had never seen a black man. They were so impressed that York was encouraged to sleep with their women so they could mix his blood with their own. That may seem outrageous to us, but Native Americans understood that diversity is a good thing, and that the more variety added to the mix, the better.

There is never just one way to do, see or know something. Diversity is the key to possibilities and survival.

5. Don't Consume More Than You Can Replace

In the autumn, when the available sunlight wanes, deciduous trees begin the process of dropping their leaves. The do this because of the economics of energy. Energy-wise, leaves are expensive for trees to make and maintain. When there is enough sunlight the leaves earn the tree an energy profit despite their expense; but when the light diminishes, maintaining their leaves would require more energy output from the trees than their leaves would be able to produce. So deciduous trees opt to shed their leaves in the fall, saving energy and creating mulch from the dead leaves to nourish the soil come springtime. (Note that trees never ask for government bailouts in order to maintain their leaves through the winter.)

This conservation of resources is built into natural systems. Bears know that they cannot find enough food during the winter to support their large bodies, so they hibernate. Other animals migrate from one area to another where food supplies are more readily available. Nature knows that to survive in the long term, an organism cannot consume more than its habitat can produce and replace. That would be like spending down the principal in a bank account instead of living on the interest. You can do it for a while, but the account will run out eventually. To last for the long term, we have to live in a way that doesn't deplete what we need to survive. Nothing in nature spends the principal in its account; everything lives on the interest.

We have operated for a long time now as though the Earth is a giant ATM machine and we can withdraw as much as we want, as often as we want, without ever running out of money. We cannot continue doing this for much longer. We are already bouncing checks against our planet's health. As our societies have grown and our technology has improved, our ability to rape the Earth has improved too. We have hunted whales to the edge of extinction using modern military-like weapons and have destroyed fisheries around the world because we won't stop and give the fish populations a chance to recover.

Early trappers in this country nearly destroyed the beaver entirely; hunters nearly rendered the American bison extinct. We did destroy many other species around the world, among them the passenger pigeon, the dodo bird, the Tasmanian wolf, the Japanese sea lion, the Guam flying fox, and…well, it's a really long list. We seem willing to kill all the animals, catch all the fish, cut down all the trees and use up everything with no regard to the future if it'll make us a buck today. Loggers in the Pacific Northwest fight for their right to continue cutting old-growth forest, though it's nearly gone. Fishermen fight for their right to continue fishing even when the fish are nearly extinct. We have to give nature time to renew herself or there will be nothing left.

When it comes to our incomes, most people will do just about anything—no matter the cost to the future—to satisfy immediate needs. We often live beyond our means, going into debt trying to maintain a lifestyle we don't need and cannot afford. Doing this ruins the future and causes stress in the present. Many of us are finding that it makes sense to pace ourselves and take life down a notch. This doesn't mean we have to live a life of rigid austerity, like a monk, or have a bleak existence of deprivation. It means that it's time to seek happiness in simpler things, and carve out a way of life that doesn't steal from our descendants' futures to keep us going today. If we can do this our tomorrows will be rich and full, if not our tomorrows may be numbered.

6. Mistakes Accumulate Over Time

If you leave Los Angeles in a boat heading for Tokyo, or in a space ship heading to the moon, and your navigation is just half a degree off, you're going to end up someplace else. The farther you travel on a bad heading, the farther away you'll be from your destination. If you have a mechanical device, a small mistake on the input side will accumulate as it passes through the system, creating a hefty error on the other end. It's a simple rule: garbage in, garbage out.

In an ecosystem, small differences—like a change in the amount of water or light, a slight raising or lowering of average temperature or a subtle alteration in the trace elements underlying the system—can have profound downstream effects. Adding something new to an ecosystem can also have significant effects as we saw in the Borneo Cat Drop, where a little DDT created a cascade of problems that got worse as they passed through the system. Mistakes may not be obvious at first, but they accumulate over time and distance.

This lesson is important to keep in mind when we make personal decisions, as well as ones that affect the future of our planet. Before we embark on a course of action, we have to take the time to think it through and make sure we are going down the truest course possible. It is important to make sure that we build room in our plans for the needed corrections that will inevitably arise. When we make a plan that is rigid, one that depends on no variables for its success, we are fooling ourselves.

We all know people who have gone into debt, perhaps to buy a house, and have worked it out so they have *exactly enough* to cover all the bills—as long as nothing changes. This is a recipe for disaster. There are always surprises. Things always change. If a plan doesn't allow room for the changes, it will collapse when changes occur.

The problems inherent with fossil fuels are another good example. We built our society on hydrocarbons and didn't make allowances for the possibilities of dwindling resources or other problems like climate change. As we continue down that road the problem becomes worse as time passes. When we find ourselves on a path that is not sustainable, it behooves us to stop, reevaluate and choose a new course, because the farther we go, the worse it gets. This is a natural fact. Are you trying to maintain a life that is built on an original bad decision? To paraphrase TV's Doctor Phil, the only thing worse than heading down the wrong path for a hundred years is heading down the wrong path for a hundred years and a day. If you're on the wrong path it's never too late to turn around. If you find yourself in a hole, stop digging.

7. Everything Is Connected to Everything Else

In nature everything is literally connected to everything else, either directly or indirectly, in a symbiotic dance honed over billions of years. We can't go in and alter one part of the whole without affecting the rest. Yet for most of our history we have operated as though nothing were connected. We have built dams, sprayed poisons, burned coal, polluted rivers and pretty much done whatever we wanted without much thought about the consequences. We only paid attention to what we could see right in front of us.

A lot of those actions have been coming back to bite us. We have discovered that we can get away with these things for a while but we can't get away with them forever. Environmental degradation, high cancer and heart disease rates, climate change and other problems have caused many of us to question the way we have been doing things. We are finally coming to realize that our decisions need to be thought out, because we have been surprised too many times by unintended consequences that could have been anticipated if we thought them through instead of plowing forward blindly. In fact, many of them *were* anticipated and warnings given, but they were ignored in the race for the almighty dollar. Our days of living unconsciously without consequences are behind us.

The connectedness to the whole in which we live goes further than one organism being connected through an ecosystem to another. It's more than just cause and effect. On a quantum level, everything in the universe is interconnected in a way makes the distinctions between you and me and that hill in the distance meaningless. Everything that exists had its genesis in the fiery hearts of distant stars, the white-hot cauldrons of creation. All matter was formed this way and has come together here in the form of you, me, your front lawn and the Rocky Mountains. Earth's thin, life-sustaining atmosphere is cycled through our bodies with every breath. The plants and animals we eat are fashioned from sunlight and earth. The energy we use passes through us and passes on into something else. Physicist John Hagelin said this: "The deepest level of truth uncovered by science and by philosophy is the fundamental truth of the unity. On the deepest sub-nuclear level of our reality, you and I are literally one."

If we can work consciously to bring this long-term, cosmic perspective to our front-of-mind consciousness, it will be easier to embrace the whole of humanity and everything else on our planet as family and help us understand that when we hurt anyone, we hurt everyone, and when we help one person, it helps us all.

8. Be Adaptable

We have all heard the story of the mighty oak that stands rigid in the storm until it snaps in half, and the flexible willow tree that bends with adversity and so lives another day. In nature, the ability to adapt is of paramount importance for long-term success. Things usually change slowly in natural systems. Ice ages come and go over millennia and continents slide around to different latitudes, carrying their inhabitants with them. These changes can take millions of years. As things change, those organisms that can adapt to the changes succeed. Those that can't become extinct.

Over the short course of our existence, humans have proven to be remarkably adaptable. We live in frigid northern climates and we live in the tropics. We thrive on the tops of mountains, at sea level, in grasslands, and forests. We are able to eat a wide variety of diets and invent tools to help overcome our challenges. These built-in attributes have served us very well over the two million or so years we have been here. When the ice ages came, we moved ahead of the ice, or adapted to it. As we moved out of our first home in what is now Africa, we adapted as we went, until we successfully populated every land mass on the planet except Antarctica. We were able to adapt to these different situations because we had the time.

Today, rapid change is happening in nearly every aspect of human life at a pace never before experienced. This change has been happening since the first steam engines sparked the industrial revolution and has carried through to the hyper-connected digital world of today. Our technology, our increased population and the resources needed to support it have made fast change a theme of our time.

In nature, rapid change can be a bad thing. When change comes faster than species' ability to adapt, it can be a death knell. We live in a world where every day surprises us with something new. Our technology had made us so powerful we can influence things on a massive scale. When we do something, it can change things in a hurry.

We have transformed the face of our planet in less than two hundred years. We have paved thousands of square miles, subjugated great rivers and changed the chemical composition of the entire atmosphere. To keep up with this pace of change we have to be nimble and far thinking. We have to adapt our thinking, lifestyles, and attitudes quickly to reflect this pace, especially when it comes to the damage we are causing, and the steps needed to stop or reverse it.

Albert Einstein once said that we can't solve problems by using the same kind of thinking we used when we created them. Our power to destroy or make negative changes that cannot be reversed is too great to operate at the old tempo, with the old thinking. A good example is the rise of nuclear weapons. When we devised these weapons, which are capable of actually destroying the planet, we had to quickly come to the realization that our old way of thinking about war needed to be modified or we could destroy everything over one transitory international squabble. So far we've managed to keep threatening each other with annihilation without pushing the buttons, but the jury's still out on this one.

In the past we had the luxury of time. We could make the changes at a natural, comfortable pace. But today the rate of change moves at a pace our brains are not equipped to keep up with. This explains in part the rise in stress-related illnesses in our society. Although change is a normal part of life, we are hardwired to resist it, especially when it's coming at breakneck speeds. And that brings us to the next thing nature can teach us.

9. Change Is Normal; Change Is Good

Yes, yes, I know. I just got through describing how rapid change can be a bad thing. But overall, change is a normal, desirable and necessary part of the natural world. I will go out on a limb here and venture to say that the one thing—perhaps the *only* thing—that we can be sure of everywhere in the universe is that change is happening everywhere all the time, from the farthest galaxy to your own neighborhood.

Strangely, despite the fact that we evolved in this same, ever-changing universe and live in it every day, change is something we resist more than anything else I can think of. We pine for the good old days, no matter when or where we grew up. We always seem to think that things were better before, and that the changes we see coming down the pike are going to be the end of us. People thought this a hundred years ago, and a thousand years ago.

Granted, the changes we are experiencing today are larger and scarier than people in the past had to deal with. But I'd like to focus now on the normal change our society—and all societies—face regularly, like the evolution of demographics, and the ongoing changes in social conventions that seem to cause so much hand wringing and consternation.

I have an old friend who is livid over the fact that so many Mexicans live in his town. He rants and raves and demands that we all do something about it. It sounds like he hates Mexicans, but I don't think that's it. I think what's bothering him is that he is seeing the world in which he grew up changing before his eyes.

If we live long enough we all experience watching the world changing into something we wouldn't have recognized a short time ago. Growing up, I didn't see more than one black person a year, except on television. Girls of my generation and before were told they could grow up to be housewives, nurses or teachers; that was about it. A woman I know who is my age was not allowed, because she was a girl, to take shop class. She had to take home economics. In my early youth schools were segregated. Blacks and whites still had separate drinking fountains in the South, and gays, well…gay people just weren't talked about. As a kid I didn't even know gay people existed. There were no female police officers or CEOs, and no blacks on television except in subservient roles. Indians were people to be killed by cowboys when they got in the way—which in the movies, they did all the time. Nobody but ex-sailors and criminals had tattoos. My America was a little Ozzie and Harriet paradise of white people being careful to not rock the boat.

In my lifetime we've gone from Ozzie Nelson to Ozzie Osborne. A woman has run for president, losing the nomination to a black man who won the election. If you'd told someone that story in 1963 they would have laughed at you. Today there are openly gay and transgender people in government and gay marriage is legal in several states. Female pilots fly space shuttles. Nice young women sport visible tattoos. The woman I mentioned before who was forced to take home economics instead of shop is now a successful building contractor in Napa, California. Bob Dylan's famous line, "the times they are a changing," remains true.

America continues to be a beacon for immigrants from around the world, but over the past several decades, instead of the majority of immigrants coming from Europe, they come from Asia, Mexico, or Central and South America. They come here for the same reasons immigrants have always come to

America; but since they are not white Europeans, they remain visible no matter how much they assimilate.

Despite the Norman Rockwell images of America that we cherish in our national psyche, the fact of the matter is that in California (where I live) and in much of the rest of the nation, in a few short years people of Hispanic descent will be the majority. In May of 2012 the United States Census reported that for the first time in our nation's history more non-white babies are being born in America than white babies. The scales have tipped. I mention this because I know that, for a lot of people, watching our nation's demographics change feels like the end of their nation as they knew it. And you know what? It is. *It's the end of their nation as they knew it.* It is now the nation as it is today.

It's a waste of time and energy to get upset over change that is inevitable. Like shaking your fist at the sunrise, it's pointless. When my old friend gets upset over the increase in Mexican Americans in his town, when people decry gay people demanding equal rights, they have to understand that these changes are inevitable and cannot be reversed. They are part of the ever-evolving social mores of our nation as we grow into the future. *It is never again going to be like it was when you were growing up.* This may seem upsetting, but to cling and fight for something that doesn't even exist anymore is an exercise in futility. To kids growing up today, this is normal. They will probably look back in 30 years and complain about how much everything has changed.

Having grown up in the sixties and early seventies when everyone was wearing bell-bottoms, I declared once that I would never again wear straight-legged pants. I held out through several fashion shifts until a girl looked at my dated bell-bottoms one day and asked if I was going to a Halloween party. In my youth, no boy could dye his hair or pierce his ear without being harassed.

Today kids wear ridiculously saggy pants; they have to hold them up just to walk. I want to say, "Hey, if I wanted to see crack like that I'd have someone over to fix my plumbing!" But it's just another passing fashion. In the fifties tough guys wore super-tight stovepipe jeans. The point is to understand that what seems today like the *only* way to do things will shift over time. Being open to this helps us be compassionate and inclusive to the quirks or habits of others. We laugh when we see old prom photos of ourselves from 20 or 30 years ago. We can't believe we wore that suit, or that haircut. Go look in the mirror to see what you'll be laughing at 20 years from now.

Recently I saw four teens laughing and eating together in a restaurant. There were two girls: one white, the other Asian, and two boys: one black and the other Hispanic. They were just four friends spending time together, but it struck me at the time (and that fact that it struck me at all is a reflection of the world in which I grew up) that this scene would have been unthinkable to some people in the past when there was so much animosity about races mixing. These four American kids had moved beyond race as a measuring stick. I smiled and felt a renewed hope for the future.

In my twenties I worked a high-stress restaurant job. When my fellow workers and I got upset over something, there was one guy who used to smile and say, "Hey, expand and include it." It drove me crazy at the time. I hated it every time he said it; but now I have to admit, it's not a bad way to look at change.

Parents and kids expended a lot of energy arguing over hair length in the 1960s. The civil rights movement was resisted by those afraid of change. Power was shifting and that always causes fear and uncertainty. Today we accept that hair length, as a point of debate, is a non-starter. Civil rights legislation is a given. It's difficult accepting change, but if we remember that it is a natural part of the universe in which we live and accept that much of it is inevitable, unstoppable and something to be embraced, we make it easier on ourselves and others. We can change our perspective of the new version of things with openness and enthusiasm.

We can expand and include it.

These are just a few of the things we can learn by asking, *what would nature do?* (Maybe we should make wristbands.) Most answers to big questions are right there if we take the time to look closely and think things through, using nature's example as our guide. There are lots more things to discover this way. We could go on endlessly learning from nature and applying it to our lives and our society, but we can't learn from nature until we acknowledge that we are part of it. We can no longer view the world as a place to be subjugated and exploited. This is our only home, and if we cannot change our heavy-handed mindset we will not survive.

On the other hand, if we start working with nature, going forward with the best interests of the planet and each other in mind, we may create a beautiful, balanced, diverse, connected, non-wasteful world to enjoy far into the future. But if we can't figure it out and end up wrecking things to the point where we don't survive, it won't be the end of the world.

No, *really*, it won't be the end of the world.

It always amuses me when I hear people say that the Earth is in danger. The *Earth* is not in danger, *we* are. If we continue our folly we may disappear from the planet forever, but the *Earth* will not disappear. The Earth doesn't care if we're here or not. If we throw things out of whack enough to destroy ourselves, she will continue on her path without us. Over time—and unlike us she has all the time in the world—she will repair the damage caused by our actions, repopulate the globe with new species and never look back.

Sara Teasdale, in her poem, *There Will Come Soft Rains*, summed it up beautifully.

There will come soft rains
And swallows circling with their
shimmering sound
And frogs in the pool singing at night
And wild plum trees in tremulous white
Robins will wear their feathery fine
Whistling their whims on a low fence wire
And not one will know of the war, not one
Will come at last when it is done
Not one would mind, neither bird nor tree
If mankind perished utterly
And Spring herself when she woke at dawn
Would scarcely know that we were gone

10

BRINGING IT ALL TOGETHER

Let us remember, our lives are but
moments in the flow of eternity, and
let us also remember that eternity
is but a flow of lives like ours.

Paul Williams, Das Energi

This grand show is eternal. It is always
sunrise somewhere, the dew is never all
dried at once; a shower is forever falling;
vapor is ever rising. Eternal sunrise, eternal
sunset, eternal dawn and gloaming, on
seas and continents and islands, each
in its turn, as the round Earth rolls.

John Muir

Infinite gratitude to the past, infinite service to
the present, infinite responsibility to the future.

Buddhist saying

We are torn continually between the needs of the present and the needs of the future. Usually the present wins because it's where we live right now, and—let's face it—in the future, we're dead. It's difficult to plan for something that you won't be there to see, and many of us expect the future to be worse no matter what we do. Someone said to me recently, "I just hope our society doesn't collapse for another twenty years, because that's as long as I expect to live." This is a fairly typical attitude, and an understandable one. Who wants to be there when the world implodes? Wouldn't you agree though that it's kind of pathetic that for many of us the best solution we can come up with is to hope we're dead before the problems we've created destroy us? Even if you're dead, your children—or their children, or theirs—will be here, and the problems we're creating today will be theirs to deal with in the future.

We don't hesitate when it comes to doing things to ensure our children have the best chance of happiness and success. It's expected that as parents we sacrifice to help them along their way even after they're grown. We work hard so we can pass down wealth, possessions, or wisdom that will benefit them when we're gone. We do this for our grandchildren as well, doting on them and marveling at the continuity of life, but what about our grandchild's grandchildren, and all their children that will follow? These are people we're not likely to meet, but they will still be our descendants, and we will be their ancestors. They will still be part of our extended family; they may carry our name. What legacy will we leave them? Are they less worthy of our consideration?

We seem only able to connect emotionally with two generations in each direction, from our grandparents to our grandchildren. Beyond that it all gets fuzzy, drifting to the edges of the unknowable past or far-off future. With our life spans increasing over the last century, more of us have been able to extend that for an extra generation, bouncing great-grandbabies on our knees or sitting at the feet of our great-grandparents. The common theme that enables us to emotionally connect with any of these generations is that *we are there too*, seeing and experiencing them firsthand. When we try to connect emotionally with generations that lived before we were born, or those that will come after we're dead, we find it more difficult.

Why should we care about the lives of those who will live long after we're dead and gone? What benefit is there in doing things in a way that will help future generations? How can we live in a way that offers the greatest good to the greatest number of people, including those of us living today? Answering those questions calls for a perspective shift. It requires us to acknowledge that *the greatest number of people have not yet been born*. As writer Michael Cronin put it, "...when we speak about the greatest good, what we really mean is the *longest* good."

We evolved with a short-term perspective that we carry with us to this day. Our brains appear to only feel comfortable when committing to the small area of the planet where we live, which includes the people in our tribe, our country, and the generations on either side of us—the *time* in which we live. But it's becoming clear that the more we cling to our perceived identity and exclude others from that identity, the more cut off we become from the world around us.

Thousands of years ago humans were attached to our band of fellow humans—our tribe. This broadened to include larger versions of the tribe, like a man in the 1700s referring to himself as a Virginian, or a New Englander. It then expanded to include an entire country—we are Americans. Even this larger view retains the tribalism and nationalism that draws lines on the Earth, labeling those outside the lines as "other."

Americans care about the future of America. We all want to think our nation has a healthy future. I imagine that most of us wouldn't get too upset if, say, Ecuador disappeared tomorrow. We would be better off to remember that we all matter. In the long run our differences are few and our similarities many. We all came out of Africa in the beginning. We are all, literally, brothers and sisters, and we are on the edge of expanding our consciousness and awareness to bridge the arbitrary and false borders we have created. We will because we must.

Our old style of thinking will not work anymore. Today with our broad reach and daunting technological power, everything that happens everywhere affects everything and everyone else. To rise above our myopia and truly solve our problems we have to embrace whole-system thinking that encompasses the entire globe, not just our corner of it. The more we let go of our "selves" the more we connect with the whole. Though our society panders to the ego and encourages tribalism and nationalism, letting go of this old thinking sets us free to pursue solutions to problems, not just patching symptoms and calling it good.

We're good at compartmentalizing our world and ignoring anything that is a remote "maybe" or doesn't demand our attention right now. We have been evolutionarily programmed to react only to immediate threats, not possibilities. Otherwise we would be afraid of everything all the time. When we see a tiger in the grass, that's an immediate threat, and we react accordingly. When it's something that we can't easily see, or don't want to see, such as climate change, we push it away. It's as though we're purposefully keeping the lights off so we can't see what needs to be seen. When we flip the light of our consciousness on, we will find the tiger is right there in the room with us. Many of us are not ready to throw the switch and shine the light on reality. We're pretending not to know, the hallmark of dysfunction. People tend to not make changes until the pain of not changing is worse than the pain of changing. We may carry a back-of-mind awareness of the need to take a longer view, but it is our habit to ignore threats until they can't be ignored any longer. The time is approaching when we will have to collectively acknowledge that we can't keep ignoring the obvious.

Is it possible to rise above our instinct to think only in the short term and reset our collective programming to embrace a longer, wider perspective? I think so, and many around the world are proving this to be true. Millions of our fellow humans have chosen a path of sustainability and long-term, whole-system thinking. There are many grass-roots organizations that have stopped waiting for governments to take the lead and struck out on their own to effect the changes they want to see in the world.

The good results they are producing are adding up, and the consciousness of the planet is slowly awakening to a new paradigm of living. The work these groups do is not reported on the news, so it's easy to believe that there *is* no good news. The media tend to focus on news that is titillating or horrifying. Sex and violence sell papers. Don't buy into it. There are millions of people working right now toward a fairer, more sustainable world. Not everyone is galloping after short-term profits while ignoring the consequences of their actions. Many are working toward restoring our wetlands, fighting for equality in workers' pay, feeding the hungry, finding alternatives to our use-it-and-throw-it-away model of consumerism and a thousand other exciting, positive, necessary things. Though their goals may differ, the one thing these organizations share is a longer, wider view of our world, our place in it and the solutions we seek—long-term thinking.

Though we are a part of nature, we can't ignore the fact that we are different from all other species with which we share the Earth and that—for us—it is possible to rise above our baser instincts. So far as we know, we are the only species with the ability to visualize the possibilities and consequences of an idea before it happens. We are the only ones who can "see" over time's horizon, the only ones who can choose a different path, though it appears to go against our interests in the short term. It's time to put those amazing skills to work.

Years ago a famous experiment was conducted on monkeys. A banana was hung from a rope just out of their reach. The other end of the rope went over a beam and hung free near the ground. If a monkey pulled the rope, the banana would move higher and farther away. Many monkeys stopped when they saw this, never deducing that if they kept pulling the rope, the banana would pass up and over the beam and fall to the ground.

Like those monkeys, humans often fail to see that while doing the right thing may appear to make things more difficult at first, in the long run doing the right thing gives us a great long-term payoff. We have to set fear aside and understand that changing things might be a little inconvenient or scary, but will reward us with a future of abundance; a future of bananas for everyone.

There is a scene in the classic movie *The African Queen* in which Humphrey Bogart plays a drunken riverboat captain who awakens hung-over one morning and discovers to his horror that Katherine Hepburn, who plays a prim missionary, has thrown his entire stock of booze overboard while he slept. He hangs miserably over the railing watching dozens of bottles of his precious gin being swept away by the river. They argue, and he pleads that it is "only human nature to drink." Hepburn replies, "Nature, Mr. Allnut, is what we were put in this world to rise above."

Rising above our nature is where the magic of new possibilities and awesome potential lies. When we use the word "natural" we mean it to describe the default, factory installed setting of things. It's natural for a stream to run downhill, natural for an eagle to hunt and for a flower to bloom in the springtime. Humans also have our natural default settings, typically set on "grab quickly," "get what's yours while you can," and "don't think about the future."

But humans also have in our nature the ability—if we choose—to reboot our day-to-day settings and select a different path. Today's global crises call out for a higher setting than our factory default. Acting in our natural self-interest has gotten us here. It's time to rise above this and strive for something *super*natural. We are talking about transformation—the transcendence—of our nature and shifting the fundamental way that we view ourselves and our world.

The flip side of fear is excitement; they are two sides of the same coin. Will it be scary to make the personal and social changes need to restore our world to sustainability? Yes, but it will also be very exciting. When we open our minds to the fact that we have to find creative solutions to difficult problems, then all things are possible. But before we can do anything it is imperative that we start thinking long term. Otherwise we will repeat our endless loops of short-term solutions that come back to bite us over and over again.

The way we're doing things today will make life harder for those who follow, and the longer we keep doing what we're doing, the worse it will get for those of us living today. It's not a secret. We consign this bothersome bit of knowledge to the back burners of our minds, where it plays an ongoing low, ominous chord of dread as a constant backdrop to our lives. We've gotten so used to it that most of us are no longer consciously aware of it. We can stop it by taking action today. When you are feeling stuck any movement—no matter how small—is healthy. As Guy Dauncy said, "Action encourages optimism."

Most of us hunger for a way to do the right thing for our planet and our fellow humans. Though we may not know how to go about it, we yearn for a better present and a better future. Vice President Al Gore said that, "What matters most is that we find one of those precious few moments in all of human history when we have a chance to cause the change we wish to see in the world...*It is time to change the nature of the way we live together on this planet.*" (My emphasis).

It's time to take our power back by expanding our vision and empathy to encompass all of humanity and as much of the future as we can imagine. Often, when faced with what seems to be an overwhelming set of problems, we shrug and say, "What choice do I have?" We ask this rhetorically. What we really mean is, "I have no choice." When we think we have no choice we position ourselves as victims, and victims feel resentful and angry. What if we asked it again, this time as an actual question: "What choice *do* I have?" When we ask this with an open mind, and ponder the ideas that bubble up, it sparks our creativity, our most powerful weapon in solving our problems.

Parents complain that their kids can't get their homework done, but they can master a video game in one evening. We say to our kids, "If you would just put a fraction of that video game energy into your homework, you'd get perfect grades!"

Likewise, if we put just a portion of the energy we expend defending the status quo or proclaiming that we have no choice into seeking new solutions, we could accomplish great things. If we take the time to form and hold a vision of the way we would like the future to look, that vision will guide us in choosing our actions today.

Of course, we cannot know for certain how any particular action or decision will affect things in the extreme long run. It has been pointed out that we can see the past but not influence it, and we can influence the future but not see it. We can, however, ask ourselves some questions when faced with decisions that have the potential to affect the long run for good or ill. Questions to ask might be: Will this be good for the whole of humanity and the Earth? Will it value life? Is it fair? Does it contribute to balance? Is it sustainable? These questions could stave off future problems but they are not often asked, especially when money or power are at stake.

Though the size and scope of our problems may seem overwhelming, the ancient proverb holds true: A journey of a thousand miles begins with the first step. If we see the world as a giant living entity, we can then imagine ourselves to be one cell in a larger system, connected to the whole. The cells in our body are hardwired to ensure the long-term well-being of the larger body they inhabit. If we imagine each one of us as a single cell in the larger body that is Earth, then if you—just you alone—decide to live in a more conscious, healthy manner by choosing those things that nurture the planet with an eye toward the future, then organism-Earth will be one cell healthier. Each time another person wakes up, embraces the long term and takes action, the planet is better off. It adds up.

Though we need to act now, we also need to be patient. The changes we need to make will not bring instant gratification. Significant societal or environmental changes rarely happen quickly. It can take decades or longer to see the effects of the shift. Nature and culture have huge mass and momentum and it's difficult to change their course. Right now we are seeing the ill effects of the things we have been doing over the last couple of hundred years. The momentum of human society has shifted toward the negative, but we can begin to steer our lumbering system in a positive direction. We don't have to sit back and watch ourselves self-destruct. It may take time to shift it again, as it took time to do the damage, but it's not too late.

Once while listening to a radio psychologist, I heard a caller asking for advice over whether or not she should go to law school. What bothered her was that if she went to law school, she would be 55 years old when she graduated. The psychologist answered, "Yes, but even if you don't go to school, you'll be 55 *anyway.*"

We often look at problems and think, *it'll take a hundred years*; but a hundred years will pass whether we do anything or not. A hundred years from now do we want our great-grandkids remembering us with disgust, or gratitude? The fact that positive change will take a long time is no reason not to do it.

How, in the middle of our day-to-day lives, with all of the franticness, bad news and fear mongering, can we maintain a long-term perspective? With everything that is clamoring for our right-now attention, how can we make long-term thinking a part of our daily awareness? First, realize that there is already a groundswell of positive activism leading the way. All we need to do is get on board. The vanguard of change underscores the subtle shift in consciousness taking place around the globe. There is much good news to be heard, and much good work to participate in. You are not alone. We live in a scary, disordered time of breathless global change and uncertainty. But as author Doug Fine said in *Farewell My Subaru*, "In society, as in physics, disorder often precedes positive change."

Second, we need to understand that the leadership we require will not come from our leaders. Governments know that when enough people draw the same conclusion, the groundswell will take on a life of its own. That's when revolutions happen. Wanting to stay in power, politicians will do anything to maintain the status quo. We can't wait for them to make the first move. In a letter to the *New York Times* in June of 2005, Theodore S. Voelker wrote, "Politicians of both parties in recent years have made successful careers by appealing to our narrowest instincts. As individuals, we have tended to punish anyone who proposes something inconvenient or suggests that we might have to make some sacrifice for the common good. In our quest to obtain what we deem absolutely necessary to our personal economic comfort, we have essentially lost any concern for the common good. Our self-centeredness makes us willing supporters of the politics of greed."

Our representatives pretend they are looking out for the common good, but their results speak for themselves. Carl

Sagan observed that, "What passes for public debate is still, on closer examination, mainly repetition of national slogans, appeal to popular prejudice, innuendo, self-justification, misdirection, incantation of homilies when evidence is called for, and a thorough contempt for the intelligence of the citizenry."

Neither can we continue to point at and blame our leaders. When we point at them we must also point at ourselves. They are in power because we voted for them. They are only able to continue doing what they do with our consent. We can't blame a president for a war, or a senator for a law, because in the end nothing happens unless we go along with it.

Adolph Hitler, while reviled as one of the worst mass murderers of all time, did not to my knowledge actually kill anyone, unless it was as a soldier in the trenches during World War I. In all honesty we can't blame him *alone* for the deaths of millions of people. He could not have accomplished his atrocities without the consent and help of millions of others to carry out his dirty work. The same goes with Stalin, Pol Pot and any other murderous despot. The prisoner abuse by Americans at Abu Ghraib prison in Iraq is a more recent example. Leaders may have put bad policies in place, but it took individuals to carry them out. We can't point anymore and say, "He told me to!" The Nuremberg defense (I was only following orders) didn't work then; and it won't work now.

No war, policy or edict, however unpopular, is possible without the consent and cooperation of the citizenry. There is power in accepting this harsh truth and finally taking responsibility. When there is no one else to blame, it leaves you and me. We can finally step up together to do what's right. Though we have to accept responsibility for all the bad stuff, we can also take credit for the good stuff and pat ourselves on the back.

So it's up to us. When our kids misbehave we sometimes give them a "timeout," so they can sit quietly and think about their choices. It would be a good idea for all of us as individuals—and as a society—to stop from time to time and reassess what is important, to see if what we are doing is working for us and to decide if the life we are leading is one that is not only going to bring us happiness and fulfillment, but will contribute to the betterment of the whole world over the long run.

In the words of Theresa Stoops, who works in environmental law in Sonoma County, California, to make any effective change we need to "inspire people to compromise." The changes we make have to be fair and perceived as good for the whole, not just a select few. Only then will people rally behind the changes and be willing to share not only the payoffs, but the sacrifices as well. Only when people feel that proposed changes will benefit everyone will they be willing to give up a little now for a better future.

We cannot continue to create wealth and comfort for only a portion of humanity. We need to bring everyone along to a better future, and make sure that everyone's basic needs are being met. Poverty, hunger, war and political upheaval all cause people to focus on the present moment. When you can't feed your kids, or you think someone's going to knock down your door and kill your family with a machete, you can't afford to care about the long run; right now gets all your attention. Part of embracing the long term is ensuring that everyone on Earth has the education, food, shelter, and opportunities they need to feel secure and equal.

Americans worry about the loss of rainforests in other parts of the world though we benefit from the destruction. We criticize those who slash and burn the forests, but before we rush to judgment we have to understand that many of us would also burn an entire rain forest or grow opium and become a drug dealer or kill any number of endangered animals, if our only alternative was watching our kids go hungry. Poverty fosters fear; fear closes minds. Fearful people hoard, take from their neighbors and fight for resources. People always take the short-term solution if they think it will keep them and their children alive, even if the lives they're saving are brutal and miserable. It is in our own best long-term interests then to lessen the plight of those in need, wherever they are.

When preparing to make a fundamental change in our actions or worldview, we sometimes hesitate because we are fearful of not knowing the outcome. In order to accomplish our goals and reach our dreams *we must be willing to embrace* not knowing. This is very difficult for us. It's one of the reasons we continue doing something we know isn't sustainable rather than trying something else. The enemy you know is better than the enemy you don't know. We want to wait before changing something until we know exactly what is going to happen afterward. If we let go of *this,* we tell ourselves, something will happen...but we don't know what. Anticipation of the unknown brings fear.

Our rational minds want to make a deal: first tell me what will happen, and then I'll decide. But we can never know exactly what is going to happen. Even when we think we know, reality always brings surprises. But to wait until we feel there is no risk is to allow fear to stop us from doing what is needed to create a better world; it's paralysis by analysis. As afraid as we may be, the "unknown"—that murky, nebulous place—is where all the possibilities, all the potential and all the hope exist.

Only when we are willing to accept that we will not know exactly what will happen, or how it's going to turn out, can we rise to the challenges we face and take the steps needed to attain greatness. This is not to say that we should act blindly. We want to make the best plans we can based on the best evidence we have, before moving forward; but we cannot let fear immobilize us. After all, what we *are* certain about is what will happen if we do nothing. It may be scary and difficult going at first, but to get moving we must learn to embrace the unknown.

Working together to improve our world and its future will do more than help those who come after us. Embracing the long term will make our own lives happier and more peaceful. When people think things are going to hell in a hand basket, their fear promotes cynicism, anger, distrust and less willingness to consider the well-being of others. Fear and a looming specter of helplessness and scarcity cause us to become less tolerant and less open to others. On the other hand, when we think things are getting better, we feel and act better. We become more generous, considerate and more tolerant of differences. Both outlooks become self-generating. We act badly;

things get worse. We act better; things get better. We cannot wait until we think things are better to start acting better. We have to start now because a positive attitude breeds the same in the world around us. We need to practice seeing the water glass as half full, not half empty.

Things run smoother when we are happy and cooperating with each other. The way we act and the way we perceive the world around us affects things outside of us. Our attitudes and desires color our reality. Knowing this, we can keep things in perspective and not get caught up in the passing drama of the moment, because anger and love are self-perpetuating. Why wait for our new world to begin? Every decision and every action adds to or detracts from the overall functionality and happiness of our world.

Remember that big drama that happened at your office or work place a few years ago, the one that had everyone upset for days? Now that time has passed you can probably look back and realize that—whatever the problem was—from your present perspective it seems like no big deal, a silly thing that happened a long time ago. It's likely you're no longer emotionally connected to that drama. Since most of the small, silly, daily dramas of our lives pass quickly, you can now look at whatever drama is currently going on and realize that in the long run it too is no big deal. You can go ahead and let go of it right now. Five years from now it won't matter, and it probably doesn't matter that much today. Letting go of small daily dramas frees you up to focus on things that really matter over the long run.

When we expand our vision and our awareness to encompass a larger view of the world and of time, we gain a perspective that allows us to live more peaceful, fulfilled lives. We can detach from the anger and frustration brought on by the daily minutia of life and focus on those things that stay true over time, nourish us and bring us peace.

Think about the things that are true for you today. Then ask yourself which of those things will still be true in a year. In five years. In a hundred years. By doing this we shed light on the fact that much of what we think is very important turns out, in the long run, to be not very important at all. We gain perspective.

In our modern world we have much to handle, much to consider and much to think about, much of the time. We ask the same questions month after month: How can I pay the rent or the mortgage? How can I afford new shoes for the kids? How can I buy the food I need and still pay the electric bill? Do I have enough gas to get to work?

Despite the difficulty most of us come up with answers to these questions month after month. We do pay the rent; we do keep the lights on. We can do this because we are creative and resourceful. When faced with an immediate problem, like paying an electric bill, we are good at finding ways to solve it. Sometimes it's easier, sometimes it's harder; but we can "answer" those questions over and over again.

Knowing that we are capable and clever enough to come up with answers to our questions month after month, maybe it's time that we gave ourselves a little more credit for our ability to creatively solve problems. Maybe it's time we challenged ourselves to ask some bigger questions. Maybe it's time to honestly ask ourselves if our life is actually working for us over the long run, if this is the direction we want to keep going. How can we create a life less dependent on fossil fuels? How can we find jobs that bring fulfillment and joy instead of just a paycheck? How can we pull back from the hyper busyness and distractions of our world and embrace a slower, more peaceful life?

When questions like these are posed to us, often our first reaction is to immediately think of all the reasons why we can't do it, whatever *it* is. I *have* to keep this job; I *have* to commute 75 miles to work. I *can't* stop doing what I'm doing, I *can't* change anything.

"I can't" is something we often say. It's never true. When we tell ourselves we can't, a mental wall slams down and shuts out possibilities, but when we ask questions with an open mind, those parts of our brains that have been so creative paying the rent each month begin to ponder the "what ifs." If I *were* to change, how would I go about it? What would it look like if I worked closer to home or didn't have a stress-filled career? How can I free myself from the fear that is the backdrop of my life? How can I make a difference in the world? How can I improve things for those around me?

When we get out of our own way and ponder the possibilities, we are often surprised at the solutions we create. When we ask bigger questions, we get bigger answers.

Some Native American tribes had a tradition of asking themselves before making any major decisions what the effect would be on the next seven generations. Thinking this way tempered their natural, human, inclination to make hasty decisions in the short term, and ensured that the passing problems and solutions of today would not adversely affect the future of their people. Many indigenous peoples had no inclination or way to measure time other than the passing of the seasons, but they had a broad sense of their ancestors and believed that they needed to honor those ancestors by showing good stewardship of their world, knowing that they too would become someone's ancestors someday.

Many of the decisions made in the last several decades not only ignored the effects on seven generations, they ignored the effects on our own generation. Who cares if we pour poison into the river, destroying the drinking water for thousands and ruining the environment, as long as I make money today? Who cares if we destroy the mortgage and financial system, along with thousands of lives, as long as there's a huge profit in it for me today?

We have put profits ahead of sanity for too long, foisting the problems of today onto tomorrow. Business interests have driven our ecosystems to—and sometimes over—the brink. We see this, but have not found the collective will to choose another path. Our fears of change, of losing something and even of each other have rendered us paralyzed in the face of oncoming catastrophe. When we do try to change things, lobbyists and corporations pour millions of dollars into protecting their own interests. Even when the damage they are doing is clearly pointed out, most fight to protect their profits. They play the fear card, and we are very susceptible to it.

I am sick of hearing that nothing can ever be changed because it would affect somebody's job. Doing what we need to do may cost some people their jobs, but we have to understand that doing nothing will cost *everybody* their jobs, and perhaps their lives. This is short-term thinking at its worst. For every good idea in the world today I guarantee you that there is a company trying to squelch it to save their profits, whatever the consequences. If this or that happens, they cry, "it will hurt my business!" But it comes down to this: If doing the right thing hurts your business, you're in the wrong business. We can no longer buy into corporate or government fear mongering. The status quo has many protectors, but the future is left swinging in the wind.

Thinking long-term helps us pay attention to things as they happen, and invites us to think about where our actions will take us. It causes us to question things more closely and thoughtfully, which helps us build consensus for future sustainability. Beware means to Be Aware.

We often have the mistaken idea that a long-term view somehow takes away from the present. We think for someone to win, someone has to lose—your gain is my loss. Everything is put through the filter of winners and losers; we are taught this from a young age. Yet many of us are finally coming to the realization that to save ourselves, we must save the entire world. The more we come to understand this, the faster the transition can happen and the better off we will all be.

Doctor Gregory Cajete is an artist, educator and a Tewa Indian in America's Southwest. His culture offers a rich example of long-term thinking. "The elders," he wrote, "remind us of the importance of the long view when they say '*pin peyeh obe*,' which means 'look to the mountain.' They use this phrase to remind us that we need to look at things as if we are looking out from the top of a mountain, seeing things in the much broader perspective of the generations that are yet to come. They remind us that in dealing with the landscape we must think in terms of a ten-thousand, twenty-thousand, or thirty-thousand year relationship."

The time in which we live was once somebody's far off unknowable future, and will someday be somebody's distant past. We are now able, even if we're not willing, to view longer and longer time vistas, and to realistically project our actions onto our descendants' future. This is a good thing if we put our new perspectives to work on a long-lasting, sustainable path.

Of course, the starting point for creating a better world is the belief that it is possible. Sometimes when looking out on the culture we have created it can seem as though it is impossible, but we have proven over and over that when we come to the collective belief that something needs to be done, we can rise to meet any challenge. We can do it again if we decide as individuals to take action now, instead of looking outside of ourselves for the answers.

When we immerse our identities in things that change, such as our job, or our pop culture, or our political beliefs, we are vulnerable to the changes that inevitably occur. Even identifying as an American—which seems like a rock-steady thing to attach to—has caused plenty of consternation to many as our country changed and evolved radically over the last half century.

Yet if we attach ourselves to the whole of the human race and the shared long-term fate of us all, we can feel at home wherever we are, safe in the bosom of our shared humanity. We can connect to the endless stream of time and the flow of life that preceded us and will continue after we're gone. We can understand that—in the end—we are more than our citizenship or our beliefs about how things should be. We are a part of something connected to the entire universe, something bigger and longer lasting than any human convention.

By choosing this perspective we can come to know our true selves as integral parts of infinity, and attach to that larger, all-encompassing reality that never changes and never lets us down. We can live contentedly and without fear, because embracing the long term allows us to fully enjoy and embrace the now. When we "look to the mountain," we can take comfort in the knowledge that although nations and fortunes may change, our place in the grand scheme of time and life cannot be altered or taken from us.

What would you do differently if you knew you were going to die in a week? Would you waste time with negative people? Would you stand around complaining about gas prices? Would you still want those breast implants? I doubt it. Wrapping our awareness around the shortness of our own lives helps us understand and appreciate just how precious is time, what a rare gift it is. Living with a daily consciousness of our brief existence can bring joy and a desire to live fully in the present and, at the same time, help guide us to act in the best interests of the long term.

I once met a man who the week before had barely survived a huge fire at the MGM Grand Hotel and Casino in Las Vegas, a fire that had killed hundreds around him. He had narrowly escaped with his life and he positively glowed with a childlike joy because of his new awareness of life's fragile nature. Elated with life, happiness and wonder, he grinned like a modern-day Buddha, infecting those around him with his joy. I only encountered him briefly many years ago, but I still remember him clearly. I often wonder if he was able to keep his newfound joyful awareness, or if he drifted back into the humdrum complacency of daily life. If all of us could capture a fraction of what he was experiencing, we would be better able to put aside transitory worries and concentrate on the things that really matter over time—life, love, charity, gratitude and the well-being of our future.

Anne Lamott has a scene in her book *Bird by Bird* that captures this beautifully. She had a friend, dying of breast cancer. One day Lamott tried on an article of clothing and asked her friend, "Does this outfit make me look fat?" to which her friend replied, "Oh, Anne, we don't have time for that."

When we go on vacation and know our time is short, we prioritize things so we don't miss a moment or waste any opportunities. We don't take our time for granted because it's limited. It's not a bad idea to live each day that way. We're all on a wonderful vacation called life, and our time, no matter what our age, is very short. This is not to say that every minute should be filled with productive activity. There is a lot to say for taking time to sit and do nothing, to stare at the clouds and dream; but when we spend an inordinate amount of time rushing from one task to the next, the hours, days and years add up. Too soon we find that we missed our life in the pursuit of things that turn out to not matter.

Think of your attention as the lens of a camera. The movie directors in our heads tend to favor close-ups, focusing tightly on that point in time that is right in front of us right now. Now let's start pulling the camera back. When we do this we begin to see the panorama of infinite time extending into the distant past and future. From our little point in time, we pan back and see the whole day, then the whole week, the whole month. As we continue, we see the years of our life extending back and our future extending forward, the billions of lives that came before us and the billions that will follow. The further we pull back, the wider our view until it encompasses all of human history, pre-history and everything since the Earth was formed, and everything that will be.

On this scale our individual lives are too infinitesimal to measure. We see clearly when we pull back far enough that our existence is but a stitch in the fabric of time's continuum. With this perspective we can smile and know that our life is not the most important thing that ever happened, but neither is it the least important. It is simply part of a grand, eternal unfolding of time and space. Things are as they are and for a while we get to be a part of it all.

Though we have to deal with the little things because the little things are what our lives are made of, we can relax and know that no matter what we think is important, no matter what we think should happen, the universe will proceed in its own way. We can fight it or enjoy the ride. It's up to us. Everything we've done—everything we will do—will disappear into the mists of time. At least three times in the past 100,000 years ice sheets have covered North America and Europe. The ice will come again and mighty cities like New York, Paris, Beijing, and many others, will be scraped away like crusty eggs stuck to this morning's breakfast plate. Our individual lives will not affect things much one way or the other in the long run, but by working together for a better world, helping to lift others and making sure our actions consider the whole of life, not just our tiny portion of it, we can improve not only our own lives, but those of every other living thing with which we share our planet, now and into the future. When the rest of the world is better off, we will be too.

When we cling to things, when we fight to keep our profits, our SUVs, our nation's superiority—even in the face of diminishing returns—we miss the point, blinding ourselves to the big picture where we are all fellow travelers, brothers and sisters, on a magical mystery tour where we all share an equal part and all share in the results of our decisions. Selfishness, greed and fear are the wrong tools to use as we build our future. We are all crewmembers on Spaceship Earth, and we all need to do our part to help keep her humming along. If twenty people are rowing a large boat together, it only takes one person putting a hole in the boat to send everyone to the bottom. Don't be that person.

And finally, we need to look at the fact that when we talk about the long run, there are two long-term realities. In the first, it doesn't matter what we do because the Earth will continue on her journey with or without us. In this long-term reality it's okay to shrug and not care what happens. Whatever we do we're going to die anyway, as will our descendants. Eventually our sun will die out and so will all life on Earth. It doesn't matter if that happens sooner or later; so who cares?

The second long-term reality is one where we care deeply about the world we will leave our descendants and hold great respect for our planet. In this reality we know we are the stewards of the Earth's natural resources, not the end users. We know that the Earth is not ours to dispose of at our whim, and understand that it's not okay to make one or two generations comfortable at the expense of the next 10 thousand. We recognize that we don't own the Earth; we are borrowing it from our children and theirs.

We each need to decide which version of the future we will embrace. If you choose the latter—as I do—then the onus for a better today and a better tomorrow is on you and me. There is nowhere else to turn. It's time for us to stop being passive observers. We have to step up and participate in our planet's destiny. We must live consciously, envisioning a sustainable future and acting upon that vision. We can start, when faced with a problem—whether a petty argument or a global crisis—by asking this simple question: *How can I make this better?*

Let us work hard to push the boundaries of our consciousness, beyond anything we've tried before, to the distant past and future. When we embrace the long term we will remember that in the middle of all the frenzied, hurried, frantic and oh-so-important issues of our lives, there stands a bigger, slower, more peaceful reality, quietly observing, never judging—simply *being.* If we take the time to sit quietly and expand our consciousness to embrace all living things and the full scope of time, we can see the kind, wizened face of the ages peering out and winking at us with a child-like smile, wishing us well and reminding us that all of this is transitory, that all truth, and all power, lie in the long run.

RECOMMENDED FURTHER READING

Allen, Craig, *Short-Term Decisions Equal Long-Term Disasters,* iuniverse, Inc., 2003

Barnett, Jo Ellen, *Time's Pendulum: From sundials to atomic clocks, the fascinating history of timekeeping and how our discoveries changed the world,* Harcourt Brace, 1998

Benford, Gregory, *Deep Time: How humanity communicates across millennia,* Avon Books, 1999

Boorstin, Daniel J., *The Discoverers: A history of man's search to know his world and himself,* Vintage Books, 1985

Brand, Stewart, *Whole Earth Discipline, An Ecopragmatist's Manifesto,* Viking, 2009

Brand, Stewart, *The Clock of the Long Now: Time and responsibility: the ideas behind the world's slowest computer,* Basic Books, 2000

Bryson, Bill, *A Short History of Nearly Everything,* Broadway Publishing, 2006

Capra, Fritjof, *The Hidden Connections: Integrating the biological, cognitive, and social dimensions of life into a science of sustainability,* Doubleday, 2002

Carse, James P., *Finite and Infinite Games: A vision of life as play and possibility,* Ballentine Books, 1986

Carson, Rachel, *Silent Spring,* Mariner Books, 2003 edition

Cornish, Edward, *Futuring: The exploration of the future,* World Future Society, 2005

Crawford, J.H., *Carfree Cities,* International Books, 2002

Darling, David, *Equations of Eternity: Speculations on consciousness, meaning and the mathematical rules that orchestrate the cosmos,* MJF Books, 1993

Dawkins, Richard, *The Ancestor's Tale: A pilgrimage to the dawn of evolution,* Mariner Books, 2004

Edwards, Andres R., *The Sustainability Revolution: Portrait of a paradigm shift,* New Society Publishers, 2005

Eliade, Mircea, *The Myth of the Eternal Return,* Princeton University Press, 1974

Fine, Doug, *Farewell My Subaru: An epic adventure in local living,* Villard, 2008

Friedman, Thomas L., *The World is Flat: A brief history of the twenty-first century,* Picador, 2007

Gore, Al, *Earth in the Balance: Ecology and the human spirit,* Plume, 1993

Gore, Al, *The Assault on Reason,* Penguin Press, 2007

Griffiths, Jay, *A Sidways Look at Time,* Tarcher, 2004

Hawken, Paul, *Blessed Unrest: How the largest social movement in history is restoring grace, justice, and beauty to the world,* Penguin Books, 2007

Hawken, Paul -- Lovins, Amory – Lovins, Hunter L., *Natural Capitalism: Creating the next industrial revolution,* Back Bay Books, 2008

Hawking, Stephen, *A Brief History of Time,* Bantam, 1998

Honore, Carl, *In Praise of Slowness: How a worldwide movement is challenging the cult of speed,* HarperOne, 2005

Horn, Greg, *Living Green: A practical guide to simple sustainability,* Freedom Press, 2006

Horn, Miriam, and Krupp, Fred, *Earth, the Sequel: The race to reinvent energy and stop global warming,* W.W. Norton and Co., 2008

Houston, Jean, *Jump Time: Shaping your future in a world of radical change,* Sentient Publications, 2004

Jackson, Maggie, *Distracted: The erosion of attention and the coming dark age,* Prometheus Books, 2008

James, Jennifer, *Thinking in the Future Tense: Leadership skills for a new age,* Simon & Schuster, 1996

Kaku, Michio, *Hyperspace: A scientific odyssey through parallel universes, time warps, and the 10th dimension,* Anchor Books, 1994

Kay, Jane Holtz, *Asphalt Nation: How the automobile took over America and how we can take it back,* University of California Press, 1997

Kelly, Kevin, *Out of Control, The new biology of machines, social systems, and the economic world,* Addison-Wesley Publishing Company, 1995

Kingsolver, Barbara, *Animal, Vegetable, Miracle: A year of food life,* Harper Perennial, 2008

Kunstler, James Howard, *The Geography of Nowhere: The rise and decline of America's man-made landscape,* Simon & Schuster, 1993

Kupperman, Joel J., *Six Myths About the Good Life: Thinking about what has value,* Hackett Publishing Company, Inc., 2006

Landes, David S., *Revolution In Time: Clocks and the making of the modern world,* Harvard University Press, 1983

Leonard, Annie, *The Story of Stuff: How our obsession with stuff is trashing the planet, our communities, and our health, and a vision for change,* Free Press, 2010

Levine, Robert, *A Geography of Time: The temporal misadventures of a social psychologist,* Basic Books, 1997

May, Rollo, *The Courage to Create,* W.W. Norton & Company, 1975

McKibben, Bill, *Hope, Human and Wild: True stories of living lightly on the earth,* Milkweed Editions, 2007

McKibben, Bill, *Deep Economy: The wealth of communities and the durable future,* Holt Paperbacks, 2007

Mithen, Steven, *After the Ice: a global human history,* Harvard University Press, 2003

Mitchell, Stacy, *Big-Box Swindle: The true cost of mega-retailers and the fight for America's independent businesses,* Beacon Press, 2006

Neustadt, Richard E., and May, Ernst R., *Thinking in Time: The uses of history for decision makers,* Free Press, 1989

Ornstein, Robert, *The Evolution of Consciousness: Of Darwin, Freud, and cranial fire—the origins of the way we think,* Prentice Hall Press, 1991

Petras, Kathryn and Ross, *Unusually Stupid Politicians,* Villard Books, 2007

Pollan, Michael, *The Botany of Desire: A plant's-eye view of the world,* Random House, 2002

Pollan, Michael, *In Defense of Food: An eater's manifesto,* Penguin Books, 2009

Ponting, Clive, *A New Green History of the World: The environment and the collapse of great civilizations,* Penguin Books, 2007

Romm, Joseph J., *Hell and High Water: Global warming—the solution and the politics—and what we should do,* HarperCollings, 2007

Rogers, Elizabeth, and Kostigen, Roger M. *The Green Book: The everyday guide to saving the planet one simple step at a time,* Three Rivers Press, 2007

Sagan, Carl, *Billions and Billions: Thoughts on life and death at the brink of the millennium,* Ballentine Publishing Group, 1997

Sale, Kirkpatrick, *Dwellers in the Land: The bioregional vision,* University of Georgia Press, 1991

Schor, Juliet B., *Plenitude: The new economics of true wealth*, Penguin Press, 2010

Schwartz, Peter, *The Art of the Long View: Planning for the future in an uncertain world*, Doubleday, 1991

Shell, Ellen Ruppel, *Cheap: The high cost of discount culture*, Penguin Press, 2009

Singer, Peter, and Mason, Jim, *The Ethics of What We Eat: Why our food choices matter*, Rodale, 2006

Speth, James Gustave, *The Bridge at the Edge of the World: Capitalism, the environment, and crossing from crisis to sustainability*, Yale University Press, 2008

Steffen, Alex, Editor, *World Changing: A user's guide for the 21st century*, Abrams, 2011

Stille, Alexander, *The Future of the Past*, Farrar, Straus, and Giroux, 2002

Symes, Jon, and Turner, Phil, *Your Planet Needs You: A handbook for creating the world you want*, 2006

Vogl, Richard, J., *A Primer of Ecological Principles*, Pyro Unlimited, 1995

Wade, Nicholas, *Before the Dawn: Recovering the lost history of our ancestors*, Penguin Books, 2006

Wann, David, *Simple Prosperity: Finding real wealth in a sustainable lifestyle*, St. Martin's Griffen, 2007

Wells, Spencer, *Deep Ancestry: Inside the Genographic Project*, National Geographic Society, 2007

Weisman, Alan, *The World Without Us*, Picador, 2007

Williams, Paul, *Das Energi*, Entwhistle Books, 1973

Wilson, Edward O., *The Future of Life*, Vintage Press, 2003

Woodward, Christopher, *A Journey Through History, Art, and Literature*, Vintage Books, 2001

ONLINE RESOURCES

Awakening
http://www.youtube.com/watch?v=QfxkFMKVAz8

Bhutan Happiness Index/New York Times
http://www.nytimes.com/2009/05/07/world/asia/07bhutan.html?_r=2&ref=world

Center for Restorative Process
http://www.centerforrestorativeprocess.com/

Charter for Compassion
http://charterforcompassion.org/site/

Common Dreams
http://www.commondreams.org/

Corporate Accountability International
http://stopcorporateabuse.org/

Future Agenda
http://www.futureagenda.org/pg/cx/view#0

General Social Survey
http://www3.norc.org/GSS+Website/

Foundation For Critical Thinking
http://www.criticalthinking.org/

Local Harvest
http://www.localharvest.org/

Longview Institute
http://www.longviewinstitute.org/

Long-Term Thinking for a Short-Sighted World
http://www.longtermthinking.net

New Rules Project
http://www.newrules.org/

Organic Consumers Organization
http://www.organicconsumers.org/organic/cuba_organic_food.cfm

Post Carbon Institute
http://www.postcarbon.org/

Project for Public Spaces
http://www.pps.org/

Saving the World
http://www.savingtheworld.net/
Slow Food USA
http://www.slowfoodusa.org/

SmartPlanet
http://www.smartplanet.com/

Society for the Deceleration of Time
http://members.aon.at/ro.neunteufel/decelera.htm

Stop Saving the World (and Start Changing it)
http://www.stopsavingtheworld.org

Sustainable Table
http://www.sustainabletable.org/home.php

Sustainable World Council
http://sustainableworldcouncil.org/

TED
http://www.ted.com/

The End of Growth
http://www.youtube.com/watch?v=XjFQLGVIJak&feature=channel_video_title

The Green Workplace
http://www.thegreenworkplace.com/

The Happiness Project
http://www.happiness-project.com/

The Long Now.
http://thelongnow.org/

The Story of Stuff
http://www.storyofstuff.org/

The True Cost of Food—The Sierra Club
http://www.sierraclub.org/truecostoffood/

The Venus Project
http://www.thevenusproject.com/

Transition Us
http://transitionus.org/home

Universe Project
http://www.universe-project.com/

Urban Food Growing in Havana
http://www.youtube.com/watch?v=jRz34Dee7XY

U.S.A. Harvest
http://www.usaharvest.com/

Wiser Earth
http://www.wiserearth.org/

World Future Society
http://www.wfs.org/

World Changing
http://www.worldchanging.com/

Your Planet Needs You
http://www.yourplanetneedsyou.org/

Made in the USA
Charleston, SC
01 August 2012